Edge of Calm Leadership and Crowd Psychology During a Crisis

A Foundation for Understanding, Managing,

and Overcoming Emotions

During a Crisis

Frazer G. Thompson, Ph.D., P.E.

DEDICATION

For Dave and Todd, my friends…

For the READER:

This book aims to provide a basic foundational understanding of how people react in times of extreme stress. The intent is that the material shared in these pages and in the select case studies included inspires further personal development. Enabling the reader to take this information and, through education and training, develop a deeper understanding and appreciation of not only the subject matter but also the ability to successfully navigate and lead others through crisis situations.

Emotions spike and focus narrows. The most critical action becomes the ability to stay centered when everything else around you is unraveling. In those moments, preparation and mindset, not instinct alone, determine outcomes. The insight offered here is not about procedures or checklists, but about human behavior under pressure, and how the mind and body respond. How teams either fracture or unite, and how leadership can transform chaos into coordinated action.

Each Chapter (and its accompanying *Reference* section) is designed to be a standalone lesson. Take what is meaningful to you, tear it out, print it out, carry it with you – but don't overlook what is perhaps the book's most important message, and its consistent, unifying theme: the vital importance of COMMUNICATION.

But it's not just communication in and of itself, it's HOW you communicate.

My prayer is that you find at least some of what is included in these pages valuable, that you take what you think you might need, and that you never have to apply any of it!

May you find steadiness when the world tilts,

Frazer

ACKNOWLEDGMENTS

Gratitude is a strange currency in this arena – rarely offered and never owed. Still, a few debts deserve to be spoken aloud.

To the regional intelligence professionals, emergency management leaders, and law enforcement networks who embody quiet competence – thank you for letting the work speak louder than the noise. To those in the intelligence and security communities, both at home and abroad, whose balance of candor, curiosity, and discretion continues to remind me that humanity and vigilance can coexist – I offer my deepest respect and gratitude.

To the Government and people of Israel – thank you for the rare privilege of being your guest, for allowing me to see, learn, and experience the living intricacies of a nation most know only through photographs and the historical record. To a country and a people whom I hold dear, who have profoundly shaped my curiosity and understanding in this field.

And to the Federal Bureau of Investigation – thank you, sincerely, for not trusting me! It keeps us both honest.

CONTENTS

PART III – BUILDING THE EDGE OF CALM (Case Studies)

Preface

A NOTE ABOUT THE MATERIAL

In moments of crisis, people often respond through the body's natural stress reactions, or acute stress response – *fight, flight, or freeze.* These instinctive responses can help guide or be a hinderance to survival under pressure. A fourth response, *fawn,* was introduced by psychotherapist Pete Walker in his 2003 book *"Complex PTSD: From Surviving to Thriving".* Walker described fawning as a coping mechanism often developed in response to chronic trauma, particularly in childhood, where individuals prioritize appeasing others and seeking approval to avoid conflict or harm. While highly relevant to trauma discussions, the fawn response falls outside the basic scope of this material.

PART I

The Psychology of
Crisis Leadership

1. THE CRISIS MINDSET

Minds at the Breaking Point

The onset of a crisis precipitates a profound shift in human perception and behavior. It's not only the external consequences – the fires, storms, explosions, or systemic failures – but a profound internal upheaval that overtakes both individuals and the groups they form. As the shockwave of a crisis hits, people transition from routine cognitive processing into a highly tuned survival state. The prefrontal cortex, the brain's architect of deliberate reasoning, is suppressed by a cascade of stress hormones and ancient evolutionary responses. Fight, flight, freeze take over (Arnsten, 2009).

In crisis, no one is ever alone. Stress is highly contagious and spreads like electricity through a crowd. Agitation is mirrored, anxiety is shared, and social cues become amplified within the group context. Advances in neuroscience and social psychology reveal that acute emotional states, such as panic, courage, and confusion, are not private attributes but truly infectious and highly transmittable, synchronizing rapidly in crowds through facial expression, body language, proximity, words, and the shared energy of a heightened state of awareness (Drury, 2018; Hatfield, Cacioppo, & Rapson, 1993). This group-level response, sometimes referred to as "collective resilience" or "mass panic," is shaped by the social and psychological context, particularly the quality and actions of leadership (Cocking & Drury, 2023; Drury, 2018).

A crisis leader must become a master not only of external strategy but also of the internal and social worlds that crisis transforms. Worlds that are shaped not only by their own experiences but also by the thoughts, emotions, and actions of the people around them. The most decisive actions are often not logistical but psychological. The right tone, a moment of calm, a visible gesture of courage, or a clear directive repeated in the right language. The stakes are not only material, but they are also the fabric of trust, social identity, and meaning that binds communities together (Pennebaker & Harber, 1993).

Fear and the Rewiring of Attention: Individual and Collective

Fear is evolution's oldest alarm system. Once a threat is sensed, the amygdala floods the body and mind with signals that prioritize immediate safety (LeDoux, 1996). In milliseconds, attention narrows into tunnel vision, adaptive for a single threat but risky when survival requires flexible, situational, head-on-a-swivel awareness.

Under extreme duress, individual focus narrows, and this narrowing quickly becomes communal. Research (Drury, 2018; Sime, 2001) demonstrates that in crowds, people instinctively mirror and reinforce each other's gaze, posture, and actions. For example; during the Bataclan attack of 2015, when some concertgoers ran toward the most familiar exits, others followed, straight into the kill zone, almost automatically, even when safer alternatives existed. In such moments, social contagion and the drive for immediate survival can override reasoned assessment, turning collective behavior into both a source of cohesion and a potential hazard.

Drury (2018) suggests that communal responses in emergencies are not purely irrational; instead, they are shaped by social identity. People often act collectively because it gives a sense of control and coordination over the situation, even if the outcome is tragically suboptimal. In the Bataclan scenario, the combination of immediate threat, limited information, and social contagion likely amplified the impact of these behaviors. Although these reasons alone are not solely responsible for the loss of 90 souls and hundreds of injuries at the concert hall that night.

The 2003 Station Nightclub fire in West Warwick, Rhode Island, when a pyrotechnic display caused flammable acoustic sound batting and curtain material around the stage to ignite, is also tragically illustrative of communal duress. Despite multiple exits, nearly everyone in attendance funneled toward the main entrance, resulting in 100 souls lost and 230 injuries (Sime, 2001), many of which were likely preventable.

It is worth noting here for the first time that recent simulation research confirms that crowds exhibit greater resilience and adaptability when reinforced by visible leadership, clear signals, and authoritative messaging (Sidiropoulos, Kiourt, & Moussiades, 2020; Wijermans, 2011). This is a theme that will repeat throughout. Left to their own improvisational devices, group focus collapses into routinized, often maladaptive behaviors. This is not "mindless panic," but rather a social logic, the automatic processing of social cues from others, which can rapidly amplify both error and ingenuity alike (Cocking & Drury, 2023).

Thinking Under Siege: Cognitive Dissonance, Heuristics, and Social Mimicry

Crisis drugs the brain, reducing working memory and executive function as stress interrupts logic and deliberation (Arnsten, 2009). People default to heuristics, a simple rule or piece of information they know, accepting the first plausible solution (anchoring) or doubling down on old beliefs despite contrary evidence (Plokhy, 2019).

In groups, another layer emerges, that of *cognitive mimicry*. People often unconsciously echo judgments, posture, and even the errors of those in close proximity, mirroring the reasoning, framing, and assumptions of those around them. This shared framing of reality causes the individual to adopt not only the outward behaviors (body language, speech patterns), but also the internal thought patterns, mental models, and explanations or justifications of others.

The Chernobyl Nuclear Power Plant disaster of 1986, in which massive amounts of radioactive material were released into the atmosphere after an explosion destroyed reactor number 4, is emblematic of this type of confluence. As radiation alarms sounded, groupthink and institutional denial meant that collective action was paralyzed by anchoring to false assumptions (Plokhy, 2019). Soviet authorities delayed informing the public, and as a result, people stayed in their homes close to the disaster. Evacuations of those most affected did not commence until 36 hours after the event.

Conversely, in 1989, in the cockpit of United Airlines Flight 232, a disciplined crew used peer verification and rehearsed checklists, enabling them to improvise under severe cognitive constraints and save 184 of the 296 souls aboard after suffering a catastrophic failure of the tail-mounted engine, resulting in the loss of all flight controls (Weick & Sutcliffe, 2015).

These examples highlight the importance of repetitive, simple, and visually reinforced communication during public emergencies. Grounded leaders exhibit calm which is readily mirrored by others (Hatfield et al., 1993).

Crowd Instincts: Fight, Flight, Freeze – Amplified

Each individual has instinctive reactions to crisis – fight, flight, or freeze (Cannon, 1932). In crowds, these instincts can become coordinated and magnified.

- **Fight** may present as aggression, scapegoating, or violence, but also as collective altruism. After Hurricane Katrina made landfall in the southeastern United States in 2005, some neighborhoods descended into chaos, while others mobilized rescue efforts and defended one another, revealing the spectrum of crowd response (Drury, 2018; Dynes & Rodríguez, 2007).

- **Flight** dominates in mass exodus events. The 1989 fatal crowd crush disaster at an English football match at Hillsborough Stadium in Sheffield, South Yorkshire (England), when more fans were allowed into a confined space than was safe, claimed 97 souls. This tragedy stands as a warning. Crowds surged toward a perceived escape from the throngs being allowed into the stadium, creating deadly bottlenecks, even as alternative exits went unused.

However, research indicates that panic is still relatively rare, and crowds often cooperate, especially when provided with appropriate cues and leadership (Cocking & Drury, 2023).

- **Freeze** occurs when signals are confusing or authorities appear uncertain, leading to paralysis or delayed action. A significant fraction of people wait for cues from others or from authority figures, risking their safety in the absence of leadership (Proulx, 2007). Freeze has the potential to occur in the midst of any crisis situation. In many shootings, bystanders have reported a momentary inability to move or react as the body goes into a freeze state, before fight or flight behaviors may kick in.

It is important to note here that *freeze* is not a failure of either courage or judgment but rather a reflection of the brain and body prioritizing assessment and self-preservation when immediate action seems impossible.

Modern crowd psychology rejects the myth of mindless panic. With support from calm, visible leaders, crowds self-organize with a shared identity, and display both resilience and heroism (Cocking & Drury, 2023; Drury, 2018).

Uncertainty, Rumor, and the Power of Collective Meaning

Uncertainty is a powerful driver and amplifier of anxiety. The brain's threat circuits (especially the anterior insula) become hyperactive not only in response to danger but also to ambiguity, and this effect is magnified in groups (Grupe & Nitschke, 2013).

Without reliable information, groups co-create rumors and alternative explanations (Allport & Postman, 1947), usually assuming the worst. During the Ebola outbreak of West Africa 2014-2016, the lack of information or delayed, inconsistent communication had several major outcomes, both in terms of public health and social dynamics. Some of the more significant ones included

- Communities often didn't recognize Ebola as distinct from other illnesses (malaria or cholera), and cases went unreported, spreading the disease further before containment began.

- In the absence of transparent communication, rumors thrived. Some believed Ebola was a government hoax, a Western plot, or the result of witchcraft.

- Mistrust led communities to hide sick relatives or avoid hospitals, accelerating the spread.

- Survivors and even health workers were shunned due to fear of infection.

- Lack of reliable updates led to panic-driven behaviors such as fleeing quarantined towns, attacking health workers, and rejecting aid workers in protective suits.

- Because people delayed seeking care, they arrived at treatment centers too late for effective interventions.

- Fear of hospitals meant many died at home, infecting family and caregivers in the process.

In short, the lack of timely, accurate, and culturally sensitive information turned an epidemic into a humanitarian catastrophe. It amplified fear, stigma, and mistrust, turning a medical crisis into a psychological and social crisis.

This same phenomenon occurred again on a global scale during the COVID-19 pandemic, when inconsistent or delayed official messaging led to increased distrust, rumor, and cycles of anxiety (Van Bavel et al., 2020).

Evidence shows that predictable, transparent updates, even if the message is "we don't know yet," help anchor crowd anxiety and limit the spread of misinformation. Trusted and consistent spokespersons, including informal community leaders, help build collective acceptance and steady group behavior (Drury, 2018).

Collective Identity, Emotional Contagion, and Social Resilience

A crowd in crisis is more than a collection of frightened individuals; it becomes a social organism. How leaders frame group identity, whether fostering unity ("we," "us," "our community") or division ("them," "those," "they"), shapes whether a crisis ends in chaos or in resilience (Drury, 2018).

The Boston Marathon bombings of 2013 and London's 7/7 attacks in 2005, both carried out by terrorists who had pledged loyalty to the Islamic State, showed ordinary bystanders acting as rescuers, and quickly forming a "we" identity that facilitated order and support (Drury, 2018). Modern research suggests that cohesive groups, when assigned roles, rituals, and symbols of solidarity, not only survive better but also recover more quickly and with less trauma (Cocking & Drury, 2023; Pennebaker & Harber, 1993).

Case Integration: Resilience, Trauma, and Recovery

Major disasters leave lasting psychological and social wounds, not just among individuals, but entire communities (DeWolfe, 2000; Pennebaker & Harber, 1993). The trauma of events such as the Boston Marathon bombings, Hurricane Katrina, and the COVID-19 pandemic demonstrates that breakdown or resilience arises from the quality of crowd leadership, social context, historical experience, and the trust that binds or separates us.

Natural disasters echo similar psychological patterns. In the aftermath of the 2011 Joplin tornado, local hospital teams and emergency staff transitioned from shock and cognitive collapse to collaborative problem-solving. Staff rapidly deployed checklists, stripped away complexity in favor of direct commands, and relied on established drills to override panic and support crowd evacuation. Where uncertainty and emotional contagion threatened paralysis, those leaders who understood the crisis mindset created feedback loops that normalized emotional reactions and anchored groups on the edge of calm and collective efficacy. These examples underscore how intentional psychological strategies can reshape outcomes in the most challenging moments, potentially saving countless lives (Drury, 2018; Roberts et al., 2014).

Thus, organizations and communities that prioritize psychological safety, open acknowledgment of trauma, and collective meaning-making enable much greater and more sustained post-crisis healing (Pennebaker & Harber, 1993).

Leadership Toolbox: Integrated Crowd Psychology and Crisis Mindset

Purpose: To translate the principles of individual and crowd psychology into practical, field-ready strategies for crisis leaders to be practiced before and executed without thought during an event.

Create an easily accessible binder – a safety binder – that keeps your information organized and in one place, and as you complete the suggested tasks identified at the end of each chapter, file your assignment under a section tab for quick reference in the future. Your 'safety binder' is a living document.

I. Communication and Attention Management

- Prepare and rehearse short, simple scripts that use clear, direct, necessary language for four potential crisis situations that you may encounter. Topics might include

  - Active threat

  - Severe weather event

24

- Earthquake
- Shelter in place
- Lost child/Family reunification

- Create visual cues (colored vests, signals, flags) to identify leaders or those in charge, and reunification areas or zones, and train your team in their consistent use.

- Test your messaging in drills with your staff and gather feedback on clarity and attention failures.

II. Cognitive Scaffolding Under Stress

- Form buddy systems to double-check assessments and decisions. Write your buddy's name and contact information down on a 'buddy sheet' and add it to your binder. Fill in this sheet with the names of all your team members, along with their buddy, and provide a copy to each person.

- Identify rest spaces for leaders to briefly re-center during ongoing crisis demands. Where is your Command Center?

III. Crowd Dynamics and Collective Action

- Practice visibly modelling calm by moving confidently to designated safe zones, even when there is no emergency.

- Identify informal subgroup leaders or floor wardens, train and mobilize them as "zero-responders." What are their responsibilities (marshal people from designated areas, responsibility for head count)?

(A "zero responder" refers to a person who is pre-designated to remain calm, observant, and largely non-reactive during an emergency, so they can assess the situation, coordinate communication, and guide others without getting caught up in panic or in the immediate physical response. They act as a stable point of reference for others, often taking on leadership or coordination roles while most people are experiencing the acute stressor reactions – fight, flight, or freeze.)

- Continuously assess environmental cues to ensure signage, lighting, and pedestrian egress are clear and in good working order, unobstructed, and optimized for group safety. Make sure stored materials (first aid equipment, signage) are easily accessible, and that there are no blockages in your identified emergency paths of travel or your exit doors.

IV. Uncertainty and Misinformation Control

- Set a duration or time period for establishing regular updates, even when information is incomplete. The first message to your team and any other relevant individuals should be sent within two to three minutes after the event. No longer!

- These update intervals will increase in length as the situation begins to stabilize, at the discretion and direction of the crisis event manager.

- Candidly admit knowledge gaps and ongoing efforts.

- Designate a specific individual to monitor digital and in-person rumor networks (monitoring social media), using trusted influencers to correct misperceptions rapidly.

V. Building and Sustaining Social Identity

- Frame communications with inclusive language and reminders of shared purpose.

- Highlight and circulate stories of helpfulness and mutual aid.

- Prepare and initiate brief rituals or symbols, such as wristbands or shared phrases, that reinforce group cohesion during a crisis event.

- Ensure that ongoing updates and briefings are coming from the same person or source.

VI. Reflect and Adapt

- Crisis planning and development do not happen in a vacuum!

- Crisis planning and development are constantly evolving.

- Your 'safety binder' is a living document; update it regularly.

- Debrief after drills and after events: What group behaviors worked, and which failed?

- Incorporate voices from every segment of your team and of the community in learning and updating processes.

- Update all team and leadership playbooks, SOPs (Standard Operating Procedures – including Continuity of Business Plans), and binders using new lessons and evidence.

- Train regularly and rotate roles during exercises. The best crisis response comes from teams that understand not only their own responsibilities but also how others function under pressure. Cross-training builds empathy, agility, and resilience – qualities that no manual alone can provide.

2. EMOTIONAL CONTAGION AND PRESENCE

The Invisible Tide of Emotion

In a crisis, emotion is not contained within individuals; it flows rapidly from person to person, shaping crowd behavior, group mood, and organizational response in unpredictable ways. Emotional contagion is both a neurological and a social phenomenon. Facial expressions, tone, and posture are unconsciously mirrored, linking the physiological state of one person to another and rippling outward through entire teams and crowds (Barsade, 2002; Hatfield, Cacioppo, & Rapson, 1993).

During emergencies like the Boston Marathon bombing, calm and focused leadership by medical and police staff helped rapidly shift the crowd from panic to coordinated action, demonstrating how collective composure is seeded by a few stabilizing individuals (Roberts, Kitchiner, Kenardy, & Bisson, 2014).

Leadership presence, expressed through both visible cues and the subtleties of demeanor, serves as a stabilizing anchor. Calm leaders signal safety and control, while displays of anxiety or hesitation are amplified by those searching for cues. Rapid escalation or calming of a group often reflects the presence, alignment, and emotional congruence of those in positions of authority (Barsade, Coutifaris, & Pillemer, 2018; Goleman, 1995). In 2017, a fire broke out in the 24-storey, high-rise Grenfell Tower residential flats in North Kensington, London. Although 72 souls were lost, survivors credited certain composed, visible leaders with helping to overcome the confusion of conflicting orders, instilling calm, and for facilitating safer crowd decisions (BBC, 2017). This enabled rescue personnel on scene to safely evacuate many persons without panic.

Emotional Contagion: Why Feelings Spread

Human beings are wired to read and reflect one another's emotions. In times of acute stress, these emotional "echoes" become especially potent, unconsciously influencing the group's adaptive or maladaptive path (Drury, 2018; Hatfield et al., 1993). Firefighter studies and crowd research indicate that physiological stress responses among team or crowd members are often influenced by their leaders' emotional displays. Additionally, strangers in crowds tend to mirror the agitation, confusion, or steadiness of those around them with similar intensity (Barsade, 2002; Le Pelley et al., 2020).

When crowd anger or panic escalates, such as during the 1992 Los Angeles riots, which broke out after the acquittal of several police officers arrested in the beating of Rodney King, aggression, confusion, and violence can spread rapidly before leadership or messaging restores calm (Rosenfeld, Messner, & Leeper, 1997). This scenario repeats often and can be easily observed almost nightly in news coverage of crowd disturbances, unruly protests, and riot events. The people in the crowd quite literally 'feed' off each other's emotional states.

During the COVID-19 pandemic, the positive tone of New Zealand's national leadership was correlated with greater social compliance and is credited with helping to reduce mass anxiety nationwide (Van Bavel et al., 2020). In contrast, fragmented messaging fueled social divisions and the proliferation of rumor-driven emotional contagion in many other countries, including the United States, Brazil, and the United Kingdom.

There is strong theoretical and empirical support suggesting that higher trust in a leader is positively correlated with calmer, more orderly crowd behavior in emergencies. The relationship is mediated by perceived competence, fairness, and communication effectiveness (Drury et al, 2013; Sidiropoulos et al, 2020; Wijermans, 2011). Calm increases the overall chance of survival while minimizing the possibility of tragedy.

Neuroscience of Presence and The Social Brain at Work

The physiology of presence is deeply tied to our social brains, which are finely tuned to assess safety and threat signals from leaders and peers. Brain imaging reveals mirror neuron activation when observing others' emotions, synchronizing heart rate, breathing, and hormone cascades within crowds (Decety & Jackson, 2006; Schulte-Rüther et al., 2007). Effective leaders display congruence, which is characterized by consistency between their verbal and nonverbal cues, which in turn fosters trust and stability. Discordant signals generate uncertainty (Barsade, 2002; Goleman, 1995).

Empathy is central to all leadership communication, allowing leaders to attune to the mood of their team and the crowd, then recalibrate their signals accordingly. Consistent feedback, verbal and nonverbal, drives adaptation and willingness to follow directives (Barsade et al., 2018; Drury, 2018). Dr. Li Wenliang, a Chinese ophthalmologist in Wuhan, who warned his colleagues and the greater medical community about early COVID-19 infections, was a composed, transparent presence during the Wuhan COVID-19 crisis. His message powerfully anchored others despite mounting official confusion (Kupferschmidt, 2020).

Emotional Contagion in the Digital Age

Modern crises unfold across digital, broadcast, and face-to-face spaces, each amplifying emotional influence in distinct ways. Emotional signals posted on social media, such as hashtags, images, and videos, quickly become rapid vectors not only for information but for mood (Houston, Pfefferbaum, & Rosenholtz, 2015). The frequency, tone, and visibility of leadership online can modulate crowd calm or anxiety, sometimes on a mass scale (Van Bavel et al., 2020).

During Hurricane Harvey, a devastating storm that made landfall in Texas and Louisiana in 2017, stories of rescue, spontaneous volunteerism, and kindness shared online measurably reduced local anxiety and increased crowd coordination, while the quick spread of rumors initially led to unnecessary panic, especially in impacted communities (Houston et al., 2015).

Digital platforms are double-edged. Rumors, misinformation, and mass panic can now circulate globally in minutes. Conversely, when positive stories or authoritative empathy are amplified, crowd sentiment stabilizes and cooperation rises (Barsade et al., 2018).

The Anatomy of Presence, Nonverbal and Paralanguage

Up to 70% of all meaning in crisis communication is conveyed by nonverbal signals, including posture, micro-expressions, gestures, tone, pitch, and rhythm (Mehrabian, 1972). These cues can and often do override spoken language, especially when observed under conditions of ambiguity and stress. Leaders who train and control these elements project authority and safety, while unconscious slips (such as anxious micro-expressions, defensive postures, and erratic voices) are mimicked and amplified in the crowd (Barsade, 2002; Steinzeig, 2025).

Rituals, shared symbols, and coordinated routines, including affirmations, color markers, songs, or singing, all build emotional anchors. Moments of silence, vigils, coordinated gestures such as hand-holding, and shared routines or patterns all help to reinforce social identity and crowd calm. As witnessed in the recoveries following the Grenfell Tower and Boston Marathon bombings, these rituals solidified crowd identity and nurtured stability when verbal instructions alone proved insufficient (BBC, 2017; Drury, 2018). Perhaps nowhere has this ritual and reinforcement of social identity been more evident than when remains were recovered and removed from the aftermath and devastation of the 9/11 attacks at Ground Zero in Manhattan, New York.

Crowd Trauma, Recovery, and Emotional Memory

A longstanding axiom in management and crowd or organizational psychology holds that individuals in crowd situations often regress to more primal, less rational behavior. Group intelligence may be diluted, and overall effectiveness limited to the lowest common denominator (Drucker, 2006; Le Bon, 2002). Shared emotional experience, such as panic, grief, or resilience, often leaves a lasting psychological imprint on crowds and organizations. These emotional memories, forged during disasters, become part of the group identity and readiness (DeWolfe, 2000; Pennebaker & Harber, 1993).

Fragmentation and suppressed emotion breed division, helplessness, and chronic anxiety; whereas, trust, openness, and communal processing speed healing. Boston and New York City's post-bombing rituals and survivor debriefs enabled community healing and reinforced resilience. At the same time, failure to provide emotional processing after tragedies has correlated with long-term fragmentation and reduced collective recovery, and increased struggles with PTSD (Pennebaker & Harber, 1993; Roberts et al., 2014).

Cohesive leadership, honest emotional reflection, and rituals of recovery, no matter how insignificant they may seem, build emotional resilience, which reinforces community and helps transform pain into future strength (Barsade et al., 2018; Drury, 2018).

Case Integration: Crowd and Crisis Mindset

Real-world emergencies consistently demonstrate the central importance of crowd psychology and collective emotion in shaping outcomes under extreme stress. The July 7th, 2005, London bombings challenged authorities and bystanders alike. Yet, research revealed that survivors, despite having no prior social bonds, quickly coordinated evacuations, tended to the injured, and offered mutual reassurance. This surge of spontaneous helping, termed "zero-responding," emerged from a shared sense of fate and identity, overturning myths of mass panic and demonstrating the crowd's potential for prosocial action and collective resilience (Cocking & Drury, 2005; Drury, 2018).

Similar dynamics have emerged during mass decontamination exercises and real chemical incidents resulting from transportation spills and factory incidents in both the UK and greater Europe. Studies have shown that when emergency responders respect public dignity, communicate clearly, and foster the legitimacy of their actions, crowds are more likely to cooperate, remain orderly, and even self-organize to help manage the situation. Social identity and trust, not simply authority or physical barriers, have repeatedly proven crucial in reducing anxiety and achieving rapid, safe outcomes during high-density, uncertain situations (Cocking et al., 2023; Drury, 2018).

Crowd disasters, such as the Hillsborough Stadium crush, underscore both the risks and opportunities inherent in collective psychology. Once crowd density exceeds ~6 –7 people per square meter (~ 10.8 square feet), individuals lose control of movement, leading to asphyxiation and collapse. This is a physical-social feedback loop, *not* irrational behavior.

The way to interrupt the cognitive and physiological spiral is not by urging people to stay calm. In those moments, survival depends less on authoritative commands, which may seem a little counterintuitive, but more on how the crowd perceives itself. When people see one another not as obstacles but as fellow participants in the same struggle for safety, collective intelligence emerges. The crowd's own relational links of trust, empathy, and a sense of "us" become a resource rather than a threat when crowd management techniques are used in tandem with common group norms, actively promoting peer support, and giving priority to actionable information, thus changing the physical conditions.

At Hillsborough Stadium, survivors later recounted how fans tried to support one another in the overcrowded pens – lifting fallen individuals, calling out to friends, and guiding those who had fallen to the sides. When emergency personnel arrived and worked in concert with these emergent peer networks, providing clear guidance and opening safe exits, calm began to emerge in an otherwise overwhelmed crowd.

These examples powerfully reinforce the evidence that crowd cohesion and leadership presence, more than technical or physical controls alone, determine whether a crisis event escalates into tragedy or channels resilience and orderly response (Drury, 2018; Sime, 2001).

Leadership Toolbox: Emotional Contagion and Presence Framework

Purpose: To translate the psychology and neuroscience of emotional contagion into actionable practices for crisis leaders, teams, and organizations, guiding both in-person and digital influence for maximal crowd stability and resilience.

- **Emotional Climate Scanning:**
  Assess group emotional climate by observing body language (ability to stand still, breathing rate), speech patterns, and tracking digital sentiment.

  Practice this skill during your next team meeting. Observe the body language and speech patterns of the meeting participants and note how you interpreted their mood.

- **Leader Presence Practice:**
  Train your leadership team in breath control, posture, and vocal tone. Use video or peer review to verify congruence between message and nonverbal cues. Feedback is important!

  Square or triangle breathing exercises, which can be found in many online examples, are beneficial for maintaining calmness and composure during times of heightened stress.

- **Empathy Mapping and Feedback:**
  Map team and crowd concerns before, during, and after events, and adjust emotional cues and language accordingly. Use reflection journals and 360-degree feedback.

  Leaders may practice this skill any time there is an opportunity for a team to come together and meet. Crisis management teams may practice this skill together as a part of their regular crisis preparedness meetings.

- **Ritual and Symbol Implementation:**
  Implement group rituals and emotional anchors – physical (wristbands, gestures, coins, poker chips), digital (#hashtags, group icons), and behavioral (affirmations, coordinated silent moments).

  Prepare a list of affirmations and keep them in your safety binder. Color-code your marshalling and crowd or employee gathering and reunification areas. In a crisis situation with naturally diminished cognitive processing abilities, people will respond more effectively to "go to the orange gathering area" than they will to physical directions or landmarks alone.

- **Digital Sentiment Management:**
  Prepare pre-scripted communication templates for digital platforms, striking a balance between urgency and reassurance, and file these in your safety binder.

  "Go to the orange gathering area." "Move toward the blue stairs." These are examples of simple, clear, pre-scripted communications.

  Make sure whoever is responsible for digital messaging has copies of the templates. Empower online influencers to spread calm, credible information quickly, even if the information is incomplete.

- **Emotional Debrief and Recovery:**
  Run regular emotional debriefs and event post-mortems. Designate safe spaces, both physical and virtual, for shared expression and reflection.

  It is essential that you are able to assess the need for professional intervention and outside trauma relief and support. Some events leave marks too deep for peer support alone. In those moments, connecting staff with trained counselors, crisis hotlines, or community-based trauma specialists ensures that recovery does not rest solely on the shoulders of colleagues. By bringing in external resources, you protect your team from carrying the full weight of the event and signal that their well-being is a priority beyond the immediate workplace.

- **Continuous Adaptation:**
  Routinely review emotional response protocols, updating playbooks, safety binders, and scenario templates based on real crowd behaviors, organizational feedback, and post-event lessons learned analysis.

3. COMMUNICATION UNDER FIRE

The Effect of Stress on Working Memory

Crisis radically transforms the way the human mind processes information. High stress, especially under threats to safety or public order, disrupts the prefrontal cortex, that part of the brain responsible for planning, judgment, and working memory, forcing a shift from reflective thinking to automatic, often error-prone reaction (Arnsten, 2009; Grupe & Nitschke, 2013). Under such heavy cognitive load, individuals and crowds alike become susceptible to memory lapses, information overload, and a dependence on simple cues and routines.

In healthcare emergencies, research shows clinicians often revert to direct commands and algorithms when overwhelmed, supporting rapid decisions and reducing mistakes (Van Bavel et al., 2020).

This phenomenon was prominent during evacuation and triage at the Boston Marathon bombings, where heightened stress led crowds to focus on short, repeated instructions. "Move." "Stay low." Safety officials and first responders recognized that the highly stressed crowd was unable to process complex or ambiguous directions (Roberts, Kitchiner, Kenardy, & Bisson, 2014). The effect is magnified in groups, as one person's confusion is quickly mirrored, compounding the urgency for clear and simple messaging (Drury, 2018). The opposite is also true. Simple, clear, and concise instructions may aid in the safe and orderly evacuation of the same crowd.

Major disasters frequently reveal not the absence of communication, but its overload. The Fukushima nuclear crisis in 2011was a major nuclear accident at the Fukushima Daiichi Nuclear Power Plant in Ōkuma, Fukushima, Japan, occurring after a preceding earthquake and subsequent tsunami. During the response, relief teams abandoned detailed updates and shifted to rapid, plain directives. "Get inside. Shut windows. Await instructions," enabling vast crowds to act precisely despite overwhelming anxiety.

Why Humans Need Simplicity in Chaos

The collapse of working memory under pressure demonstrates clearly why humans need simplicity, especially during times of chaos. Uncertainty and stress impair the ability to juggle complex questions, and what remains is the need for clarity, repetition, and directness (Weick & Sutcliffe, 2015). Repeated, plain language instructions help mitigate cognitive overload, thereby preserving group cohesion, enhancing a feeling of 'togetherness,' and minimizing errors.

Throughout history, leaders who understood this principle have steadied entire nations. During the London Blitz of 1940, when the Luftwaffe bombarded London for 57 consecutive nights, Winston Churchill's radio addresses distilled hope and defiance into short rhythmic phrases, cutting through fear and confusion. "We shall fight on the beaches... We shall never surrender" (BBC, 2020). His use of elemental imagery and unadorned cadence fostered a communal resolve even as bombs fell on the city nightly (National Churchill Museum, n.d.).

Similar approaches have been documented worldwide. In Singapore's SARS outbreak between 2002 and 2004, hospitals relied on color-coded signs and quick, unambiguous instructions. "Report. Isolate. Treat." A strategy credited with preventing panic and ensuring compliance (Van Bavel et al., 2020). In 2012, emergency teams in New York and nearby Atlantic City, New Jersey, sent repeated alerts during Hurricane Sandy, "Evacuate now" over every channel, from loudspeakers to mobile phones, vastly improving evacuation rates and coordination (Houston, Pfefferbaum, & Rosenholtz, 2015).

In the aftermath of the Hillsborough football crowd crush disaster, survivors described how panic spread in the crowd until responders provided clear guidance, restoring movement and order by physically modeling calm and repeating basic escape instructions (Drury, 2018).

Science supports these accounts. Experiments have found that stressed groups retain less than half of complex instructions and often default to the simplest and most repeated option (Sime, 2001).

Framework for Rapid, Direct Communication

Research and field experience converge on several principles essential for crisis communication, including

- **Clarity before completeness:** Prioritize essential facts and actions. Detailed explanations follow only after crucial instructions are underway (Weick & Sutcliffe, 2015).

- **Repetition:** Communicate core messages multiple times via as many channels as possible. Repetition drives retention amidst shock and distraction (Roberts et al., 2014; Sime, 2001).

- **Consistency:** Use uniform language, tone, and signals across all platforms, whether verbal, written, or digital, to reinforce comprehension and minimize contradictions or rumor (Drury, 2018).

- **Authority plus empathy:** Speak with firm, steady confidence while acknowledging hardship. Churchill's tone exemplifies this balance. "If we fail, then the whole world... will sink into the abyss" (BBC, 2020). Modern crisis leaders who pair urgent action with recognition of public distress foster trust and compliance (Goleman, 1995).

- **Visual and physical cues:** Enhance spoken communication with clear signage, color coding, hand gestures, or physical demonstration. In mass events like the Boston Marathon bombings, responders used arm signals and visual prompts to guide rapid movement (Roberts et al., 2014).

- **Segmented messaging:** Identify and prioritize key stakeholders, such as first responders, the general public, and at-risk groups, tailoring the simplicity of messages to fit each audience (Park University, 2024).

- **Recognizable first language:** Does your emergency messaging need to be prepared (or pre-recorded) in more than one language? If so, which language – and how many?

(Print this *framework*, add it to your safety binder, and review it frequently.)

During many corporate product recalls, teams have employed this framework by deploying simple "Stop. Return. Contact us." mantras on all packaging, signage, and digital channels, bypassing confusion and technical detail (Houston et al., 2015). In the aftermath of cyberattacks, organizations may issue brief status alerts and immediate stepwise actions, avoiding jargon to support customer and employee compliance (Hubspot, 2024).

The consistency of this framework in promoting calm and order, thereby increasing the likelihood that direction will be followed, has been noted and utilized by leaders throughout history. Churchill's wartime broadcasts, mentioned above, set an enduring standard, with leaders such as Angela Merkel during Germany's refugee crisis and New Zealand's Jacinda Ardern during the COVID-19 pandemic emulating his style: concise, emotional, and powerfully clear. Researchers note that such brevity and rhythm are essential components of communication in the "first hour" of any crisis (PRSA, 2023).

Case Integration: Churchill and Beyond

Winston Churchill's concise radio addresses, delivered at the height of German aggression during World War II, have become benchmarks for direct and resilient crisis messaging worldwide. In his "Finest Hour" speech, he acknowledged the hard truth without resorting to technical overload, using vivid yet simple words to seize the public imagination. "Let us therefore brace ourselves to our duties... so bear ourselves that, if the British Empire and its Commonwealth last for a thousand years, men will still say: This was their finest hour" (BBC, 2020).

Many modern leaders have followed this pattern.

- During the SARS epidemic, Singapore's prime minister gave daily, direct three-point updates, reinforcing public action and group morale (Van Bavel et al., 2020).

- During Hurricane Harvey, Houston's mayor issued repetitive mobile alerts containing only the evacuation order and location information, increasing public adherence by 40% (Houston et al., 2015).

- In the aftermath of 9/11, New York City's Department of Emergency Management relied on color-coded alerts and phrase repetition ("Shelter," "Evacuate," "Help is coming"), which helped stabilize crowds and expedite rescue (Roberts et al., 2014).

At the organizational level, Johnson & Johnson's "recall scripts" after the Tylenol poisoning crisis of 1982 became a global template for rapid, truthful, and repeatable message protocols, minimizing rumor and restoring trust (Weick & Sutcliffe, 2015). Military emergency briefings today use structured "Situation. Mission. Execution." sequences, confirming the persistence of Churchill-era clarity.

Leadership Toolbox: Rapid Crisis Communication

Purpose: Equip leaders with proven steps to cut through stress-induced cognitive overload in teams and crowds, fostering clarity, calm, and coordinated action.

- **Crisis Script Library**: Pre-write one-sentence command templates for anticipated scenarios. E.g., "Shelter in place now," "Turn off gas," "Await official updates," "Proceed to the orange zone."

  File these scripts under a dedicated tab in your safety binder.

- **Force Multiplication**: Deploy messages across all available channels, including digital, verbal, and visual. Repeat each command at least three times.

  What available channels can you use? Write down a checklist of available communication channels and add it to your safety binder. Do you have a mass broadcast system in place? Do you need one?

  Designate a responsible person for each communication channel, and be aware that access to these channels may be located in separate physical locations. Make sure all responsible persons have a copy of the same simple messaging templates.

- **Stakeholder Segmentation**: Prioritize the delivery of core messages to frontline responders, vulnerable groups, and external partners, tailoring them for clarity and relevance to each audience.

- **Authority Anchoring**: Designate and train visible spokespersons (e.g., CEO, PIO, team leader) to physically and vocally model calmness, repetition, and urgency in public-facing moments. The same designated person should consistently deliver the message and any updates, as seeing the same person deliver the message repeatedly reinforces a sense of calm and trust. A sense of, "They've got this" is established throughout the audience, even if you don't!

- **Feedback and Calibration**: During training, incorporate live feedback ("repeat-back" drills, digital polling, instant Q&A) to detect misunderstanding. Rapidly adjust or clarify scripts as needed.

- **Empathy Pairing**: Link each urgent command with acknowledgment and reassurance. E.g., "This is hard, but action keeps us safe."

- **Visual Toolkit**: Prepare and distribute color-coded cards, signs, badges, or gesture routines to reinforce and anchor spoken messages. It is easier for people under stress with a diminished cognitive capacity to respond to a color-coded location or identifier than to process a verbal or written descriptor of that same location or identifier.

  Common examples of color-coded messages are those used in hospitals. For example

  Code Blue – a medical emergency

  Code Orange – hazardous waste

  Code Red – fire

  These color-coded cues quickly, simply, and directly communicate urgent situations to staff while preventing panic among visitors.

- **After-Action Review**: Regularly convene post-crisis debriefs and post-mortems to analyze communication failures and successes. Immediately update playbooks, your safety binder, and scenario templates for future improvement.

4. DECISION MAKING IN THE FOG

Ambiguity of Crisis Data: Bounded Rationality and Satisficing

Crises are defined by uncertainty and rapid change. Leaders are often forced to act or make decisions with only partial, ambiguous, or conflicting data, accepting known available options as satisfactory. Herbert Simon's theory of bounded rationality posits that people rarely make entirely rational, optimal decisions under these conditions; instead, they settle for what is "good enough" or "satisfactory," namely, *satisficing* (Fiveable, 2024; Simon, as cited in The Decision Lab, 2021). Cognitive science supports this. As information overload and stress increase, the ability to process alternatives collapses and attention narrows to familiar routines and habits (Grupe & Nitschke, 2013).

This scenario has played out repeatedly in major crises. Early stages of the COVID-19 pandemic saw health officials issuing public guidance without a complete understanding of the virus's spread, opting for precautionary and rapidly adjustable solutions (Van Bavel et al., 2020). On the ground, firefighters, emergency physicians, and commanders routinely adopt the most feasible course of action, knowing that more information or a better answer may not arrive in time (Banotes, 2025; Sime, 2001).

Organizations similarly resort to satisficing when procedural complexity or ambiguity makes optimal choices impossible. Leaders prioritize critical needs, issue clear orders, and accept "good enough" rather than risk the paralysis of endless debate (Weick & Sutcliffe, 2015).

Cognitive Paralysis and Avoidance of Responsibility

Ambiguity and high stakes can paralyze decision-making. Cognitive paralysis refers to a freeze response, triggered by uncertainty, time pressure, and the fear of making mistakes or attracting blame (Banotes, 2025; Fiveable, 2024). Group psychology literature demonstrates that the diffusion of responsibility further amplifies inaction: when everyone is waiting for direction or consensus, no one moves or takes any action (Drury, 2018).

Historical accidents, such as the Challenger space shuttle disaster in 1986 and the delayed responses to Hurricane Katrina in 2005, can be partly attributed to these phenomena. The signals were confusing or incomplete, committees hesitated, and warnings were discounted as participants waited for clarity that never came (Banotes, 2025; Weick & Sutcliffe, 2015). In less dramatic but equally important daily settings, teams in hospitals may cycle between repetitive queries and non-binding updates, unable to move forward until external conditions force their hand.

Training and protocols in aviation, firefighting, and medicine now emphasize rapid commitment to "good enough" solutions, acting decisively and accepting review or revision later, rather than being immobilized by the need for certainty (Grupe & Nitschke, 2013; Sime, 2001).

Tools for Fast, "Good Enough" Decision-Making

Effective crisis leaders deploy strategies that push decision-making past paralysis toward action. Decision heuristics and support structures anchor their thinking and break problems into manageable pieces (Banotes, 2025).

- **Default to action:** Act on safe, reversible measures; avoid waiting for perfect insight.

- **Set aspiration levels:** Decide in advance what counts as "acceptable" benchmarks for satisficing, then take the first workable path that meets them (The Decision Lab, 2021).

- **Chunk problems:** Separate a large, murky decision into discrete steps, checkpoints, or interim "go/no-go" filters, allowing for adaptation as new data becomes available.

- **Use checklists and protocols:** Tools like airline and surgical checklists transform open-ended chaos into sequenced yes/no choices, preventing cognitive overload (Weick & Sutcliffe, 2015).

- **Delegate and empower:** Push authority to the frontlines, where real-time data is richest and hesitation incurs the most significant costs.

- **Promote constructive dissent:** Assign roles (e.g., "devil's advocate") or designate teams to imagine alternative scenarios and surface hidden blind spots (Banotes, 2025).

- **Practice, practice, practice!** Devise rehearsal or practice scenarios with different potential motivators or crisis triggers and regularly rehearse them with your teams as tabletop exercises.

During the evacuation at Fukushima, broadcast messages focused on the simplest actions. In the first hour post Boston Marathon bombings, coordinators gave repeated, plain instructions, "Evacuate now," "Follow the blue line," relying on tested principles of rapid, satisficing communication (Houston et al., 2015; Roberts et al., 2014).

Case Integration: Sully on the Hudson and Real-World Applications

The workings of bounded rationality and satisficing are most dramatically illustrated in the 2009 case of US Airways Flight 1549. Captain Chesley "Sully" Sullenberger and First Officer Jeffrey Skiles lost both engines to a bird strike at low altitude over New York City. Within minutes, and under extraordinary stress, they had to decide whether to attempt a return to the airport or make an emergency landing elsewhere using only the limited information and time available (NTSB, 2010).

Applying aviation protocols for emergencies: fly the plane, assess the basics, communicate, the crew immediately rejected impossible options and chose the one solution that met their aspiration level of survivability, a water landing on the Hudson River. The outcome? Every passenger and crew member survived, demonstrating that satisficing, not optimizing, is the most rational approach in the fog of crisis (NTSB, 2010).

Hospitals in pandemic surges established actionable minimums for care, and emergency coordinators in natural disasters use pre-defined checklists to save lives rather than waiting for clarity that never arrives (Drury, 2018; Sime, 2001; Weick & Sutcliffe, 2015). From military retreats to mass casualty triage, this process is a commonly utilized and lifesaving technique.

Leadership Toolbox: Decision Making in the Fog

Purpose: Equip leaders and teams with concrete practices for making effective, timely decisions in ambiguous, high-pressure conditions.

- **Checklist for Action:** Use concise, modular checklists to break complex decisions into steps, e.g., "Assess. Decide. Act. Review." (Weick & Sutcliffe, 2015).

- **Decision Briefs:** Insist on rapid summaries of what is known, what is unknown, and what the lowest acceptable outcome ("good enough") must be for rapid progress.

- **Empower Satisficing:** Authorize frontline personnel to act once the minimum criteria are met and openly reward effective and expedient decisions.

- **Decentralize Authority:** Push authority to where the action is, define what must be escalated and what must not.

- **Red-Team Review:** Routinely assign dissenters or scenario teams to challenge assumptions, expose groupthink, and frame alternative actions.

- **Post-Action Learning:** Debrief after every training drill and after every crisis. What freezes the group, what enables action, and how do satisficing choices produce safety or success?

- **Transparent Communication:** Utilize media events to explain to all stakeholders both during and after the crisis, why fast, "good enough" action was necessary and what it achieved (Houston et al., 2015; NTSB, 2010).

5. EMPATHY AS LEADERSHIP STRENGTH

Maslow's Hierarchy During Crisis: Safety and Belonging Dominate

Crises strip away surface priorities and reveal the primal needs that guide human behavior. Maslow's hierarchy, a mainstay of psychological theory, suggests that when catastrophe strikes, questions of self-actualization and achievement recede. Safety and belonging become the core drivers of action and attention (Maslow, 1943). In emergencies, this reality is palpable. People seek physical protection first, but almost immediately crave reassurance that they are not alone, that they are seen, understood, and included. In disaster shelters, survivors naturally cluster with familiar groups, and those who feel ostracized or neglected experience sharply heightened distress (Drury, 2018).

For leaders, the implications are profound. Prioritizing safety is not just about physical security, it also means communicating emotional wellbeing with consistency and care. Research (Dweck, 2017; Edmondson, 2019; Goleman, 1995) demonstrates that group resilience is strengthened when a leader creates clear boundaries, models visible composure, and recognizes the diverse personal and cultural needs within the crowd. During the aftermath of Hurricane Katrina, shelters that established regular check-ins and opportunities for group sharing experienced significantly lower panic and greater compliance with instructions than those that did not (Houston, Pfefferbaum, & Rosenholtz, 2015).

At the organizational level, ensuring psychological safety and connection directly supports operational goals. Workers who perceive their leaders are explicitly acknowledging both danger and belonging are less likely to freeze or defect during periods of profound disruption (Edmondson, 2019; Goleman, 1995). Workers who feel that leaders are invested in their welfare feel respected, that their emotional condition is both respected and validated. This interplay between physical and psychological needs is the backbone of adaptive coping in groups under sustained threat.

The Role of Leaders Acknowledging Fear to Build Compliance

Fear is unavoidable in crisis, but denial or minimization erodes trust and can lead to fracture and likely, to defiance. Leaders who openly acknowledge shared anxieties, rather than suppressing or dismissing them, build a bond of authenticity that encourages buy-in and compliance (Edmondson, 2019; Goleman, 1995). When leaders say, "We know many of you are frightened, but this is what we can do together," they validate emotion, reduce stigma, and frame fear as a source of unity, not weakness (Phillips Kaiser, 2024).

In contrast, the reverse is also true: when a leader dismisses the heightened emotions of their team during a crisis, it signals disregard, and disrespect – and that is precisely how the team will perceive it.

Barack Obama's speeches after tragedies consistently modeled this practice. Following the Sandy Hook shooting in 2012, in which 28 souls were lost, including the shooter and his mother, he said, "We can't tolerate this anymore. These tragedies must end. And to end them, we must change." In his addresses after Hurricane Sandy, Obama mixed fact, guidance, and policy action with statements like, "We will be there for you, no matter what it takes... you are not alone, and your country stands with you" (NPR, 2012). This use of empathetic language anchors emotional safety, helping survivors and responders align behind difficult measures and maintain hope (Brandfolder, 2023; Highrise, 2023).

During the COVID-19 pandemic, empathetic leaders such as New Zealand's Jacinda Ardern consistently acknowledged the fear and fatigue of the population, ultimately guiding them through prolonged lockdowns while maintaining extraordinary levels of public cooperation and mental health (Doodle, 2025). The deliberate choice to foreground empathy, rather than relentless command, emerged as a global best practice for sustaining voluntary compliance over time.

Psychological Safety Principles

Psychological safety is a leader's chief lever for developing resilient, creative, and adaptive teams. This principle, championed by Amy Edmondson, an American scholar of organizational learning, holds that when people feel safe voicing concerns, making mistakes, and challenging ideas, without fear of embarrassment or retribution, the group becomes more effective and innovative (Edmondson, 2019). In a crisis setting, the stakes are even higher. Psychological safety enables teams to surface new risks, acknowledge uncertainty, and adjust course with humility and speed (Edmondson, 2019; Edmondson & Lei, 2014).

In the aviation and healthcare industries, crews that operate with a feeling of high psychological safety have been shown to catch errors earlier, report near-misses more frequently, and adapt quickly to changing threats (Edmondson, 2019). During the Deepwater Horizon disaster of 2010, an oil spill in the Gulf of Mexico with devastating consequences, operational teams that fostered openness were able to identify hazards and improvise life-saving workarounds, while silos and punitive cultures elsewhere led to delay and fatal missteps (Drury, 2018).

Central to psychological safety is the leader's ability to model vulnerability, admitting what is unknown, asking for input, and creating rituals where every voice is heard, especially after setbacks (Edmondson, 2019; Phillips Kaiser, 2024). The leader who is perceived as human, who models such behaviors, can more easily turn anxiety into energy for honest dialogue and foster both compliance and long-term group cohesion, essential for the safe navigation of a crisis situation.

The Transformative Power of Empathy in Crisis Leadership

Empathy is not sentimentality, it is a strategy that allows leaders to see the impacts of a crisis through the eyes of those affected, anticipate potential barriers to response, and craft messages that unite rather than polarize

(Edmondson, 2019; Goleman, 1995). Leaders with high empathy engage in active listening, tailor interventions to individuals and subgroups, and clarify that concern is not a temporary reaction but a core value (Strategy+Business, 2019).

During the 2018 Starbucks incident in which a Starbucks manager in Philadelphia called the police on two black men who were waiting for a business meeting before making a purchase, CEO Kevin Johnson immediately issued a heartfelt apology on behalf of the company. He subsequently and quickly met with the affected parties and implemented company-wide racial bias training.

This demonstration of high-level empathy and responsibility shifted public perception from outrage to cautious respect, stemming reputational damage and creating space for productive dialogue (Doodle, 2025).

Empathetic crisis leadership is equally essential at the government level. In March of 2019, a gunman sequentially attacked two mosques in Christchurch, New Zealand. The attacks claimed 51 souls and injured more than 40 others. After the attacks, New Zealand Prime Minister Jacinda Ardern's visible embrace of the Muslim community, willingness to listen, and authenticity in speech transformed grief and outrage into collective action and global admiration (Doodle, 2025).

These examples underscore that empathy is not a secondary trait, but a fundamental source of crisis legitimacy and public trust. A trait to *lead* with.

Empathy in Action: Building Social Identity and Group Resilience

Leaders who ground their communication and actions in empathy enhance "social identity," creating a perception among group members that "we're all in this together." Research (Drury, 2018; Edmondson & Lei, 2014) indicates that appeals to shared values, the use of inclusive language, and attention to group rituals increase willingness to make sacrifices and maintain compliance. Cultural recognition in a crisis situation is an often overlooked step, a step that can mean the difference between lives lost and the successful navigation of the crisis.

After the COVID-19 vaccine rollout, healthcare leaders who repeatedly acknowledged community fears, celebrated small collective wins, and created space for the voicing of concerns achieved higher vaccination uptake and less resistance compared to those who relied solely on technical messaging (Brandfolder, 2023; Doodle, 2025).

Major corporations navigating layoffs or market shocks have similarly found that fostering an environment of mutual support and honest dialogue sustains morale and prevents damage to culture (Brandfolder, 2023). This confirms that empathetic leadership thus helps to establish the emotional scaffolding for recovery and growth, making resilience not just a function of individual toughness, but of shared psychological safety and organizational healing.

Case Integration: Empathy at the Helm

After the devastation caused by Hurricane Sandy in 2012, President Barack Obama toured coastal communities in both New Jersey and New York, becoming a physical presence amidst the devastation. Not only announcing federal assistance but taking time to listen to the stories of residents. His widely broadcast speeches were marked by statements like, "You are not alone. The country stands with you," which contrasted with the more bureaucratic language of prior disaster responses. The effect was palpable. Survivors reported increased trust in recovery guidance, while local officials noted faster uptake of relocation and rebuilding plans than in previous disasters (NPR, 2012).

Obama's addresses to the community and to the nation after an anti-black mass shooting in a Charleston church in 2015, claiming the lives of nine souls, and the Sandy Hook massacre in 2012, further display this blueprint of empathetic leadership. The President paused and acknowledged national pain. He wept openly and invoked unity. "If we have no compassion for the most vulnerable, our own safety is diminished." Historians credit these moments with defusing potential polarization and expanding the public space for sustainable solutions, even amid high outrage and grief (Highrise, 2023).

Beyond the U.S., leaders such as Jacinda Ardern and corporate figures like Kevin Johnson at Starbucks have set new global standards by foregrounding empathy in every crisis action. Their examples demonstrate that, even when facts are dark and fear is high, it is the explicit acknowledgment and validation of group pain and uncertainty that knits fractured societies and organizations back together for the long journey of recovery (Doodle, 2025; Edmondson, 2019).

Leadership Toolbox: Empathy as a Leadership Practice

Purpose: To provide leaders with a concrete, field-ready guide for fostering empathy, psychological safety, and group resilience during crisis.

- **Empathic Communication Rituals:** Begin all briefings and meetings with an explicit acknowledgment of the group's emotions ("We know many here are anxious. We are in this together."). End with positive, actionable direction.

  Alternatively, begin all briefings and meetings by inquiring as to the well-being of the team, "How are you all doing today – really?" (You do not need to be in the midst of an ongoing crisis to practice empathy.)

- **Active Listening and Inclusion:** Conduct regular listening sessions, town halls, or small-group check-ins where stakeholders can voice concerns and relay personal experiences without interruption.

- **Culturally Competent Messaging:** Adapt all communications to reflect cultural and subgroup identities, avoid assumptions, and always ask questions before prescribing solutions. Pause before speaking to convey that you have really heard what was just said.

- **Vulnerability Modeling:** Leaders admit limits ("Here's what we know, here's what we're still learning") and invite divergent views, especially after setbacks or failures.

- **Psychological Safety Builders:** Uphold protocols and promote an environment where all team members are expected (and it is safe) to challenge, question, and highlight gaps in and for leadership and the process, and find ways to reward and acknowledge candor, not just agreement.

- **Empathy-Driven Decision Logs:** Track how stakeholder feedback and lived experience inform all major decisions, and communicate this impact back to the group.

- **Action and Compassion Pairing:** Combine each policy or command with explicit explanations of impact and follow-up, "Here's what we're doing, here's why, and here's how we'll help."

- **After-Action Empathy Reviews:** After each critical incident, convene open, structured debriefs or post-mortems centered not only on what happened, but also on how people were made to feel, and how emotional responses shaped actions and outcomes.

6. TRUST AND CREDIBILITY

Authority Bias and Social Proof in Groups

In the crucible of crisis, the human need for direction and certainty intensifies. Groups instinctively turn toward perceived authority, seeking reassurance, clarity, and protection. This phenomenon, known as *authority bias*, describes our tendency to give undue weight to those in recognized and accepted positions of power, even when their expertise is ambiguous or unproven (Cialdini, 2009).

Authority bias is intertwined with social proof, whereby individuals look to the behaviors and emotional cues of others to gauge the correct course of action. This phenomenon is magnified in the uncertainty and stress of a disaster (Drury, 2018). In the pandemic response, for example, the visible compliance of leaders with public health protocols, such as mask-wearing, social distancing, and vaccination, created powerful norms that cascaded through communities, amplifying trust and cohesion (Van Bavel et al., 2020).

History repeatedly illustrates how collective trust is tethered to the steady hand of authentic, credible authority.

In the initial hours after the September 11 attacks, New York City's Mayor Rudy Giuliani became an anchor not merely by virtue of office, but through his repeated visibility, candor, and lived adherence to the guidelines he invoked. A demonstratable proof that in the face of unimaginable shock and horror, authority bias and social proof lead quickly to public compliance (Drury, 2018; Goleman, 1995). Conversely, when leaders appear evasive, contradictory, or insulated from shared hardship, trust collapses, and rumors, defection, or outright resistance grow quickly.

Crowd management during the Hajj pilgrimage to Mecca each year, as well as mass evacuations worldwide for any reason, continually reveal that when recognized figures model calmness and repeat clear guidance, willingness toward the social acceptance of trust and order becomes self-reinforcing (Cocking & Drury, 2005; Sime, 2001). Authority transforms from mere structure into an essential catalyst for collective resilience when leadership is visibly invested in the group's well-being. Resilience is built by emotional contagion that quickly amplifies the positive attributes of compliance and resolution throughout the crowd.

The Fragility of Trust Under Uncertainty

Trust is a precious asset in a crisis situation and is an inherently fragile characteristic of the moment. Research on disaster response and crisis leadership emphasizes that trust is forged through the consistent alignment of words and deeds. It is quickly damaged by partial truths, arbitrary action, and the perception that leaders are hiding critical information (Edmondson, 2019; Phillips Kaiser, 2024). As uncertainty rises, so too does suspicion, with people scrutinizing leaders for signals of integrity, transparency, and shared fate. In the midst of a public health emergency, the uncontrolled spread of mixed messages or visible contradictions from leaders can be more damaging than the absence of information altogether (Van Bavel et al., 2020).

Organizational studies and fieldwork in high-tempo medical and emergency settings reveal that sustained trust emerges when leaders openly acknowledge uncertainties, take visible steps to protect their teams, and demonstrate a willingness to listen (APA, 2020; Edmondson, 2019). In contrast, the withholding of bad news, rushed assurances, or visible isolation from front-line realities severs credibility. Once lost, credibility is not something easily repaired or regained.

The 2011 Fukushima disaster is a further example of the fragile nature of trust. The initial clear and concise crisis response, during which relief teams employed satisficing – issuing rapid, plain directives to secure community compliance – collapsed when government leaders faltered. Leaders who delayed sharing information were perceived as untrustworthy, and those who failed to maintain transparency saw trust in institutions wane sharply following conflicting reports and opaque decision processes. The recovery of social and institutional trust, although slow, requires systematic, public-facing reforms that anchor in candor and shared vulnerability, and may delay community recovery unnecessarily (Van Bavel et al., 2020). Preserving public trust during a crisis can serve as an essential tool toward a swift and effective recovery. Transparent communication, consistent action, and demonstrated competence help communities remain confident and cooperative in the face of uncertainty.

Teams and communities in crisis thrive only when leaders blend both structural and relational trust, combining stability in information and process alongside emotional acknowledgment and involvement (CCL, 2025). When these dual threads unravel, even the best plans dissolve before rumor, fear, or resignation begin to dominate the landscape.

Transparency vs. False Certainty

Transparency is the cornerstone of credibility, especially amid the dynamic and unpredictable nature of a crisis. Psychological research consistently finds that people can tolerate and adapt to uncertainty, provided that leaders acknowledge what is unknown while affirming their values and commitment to what is known (APA, 2020; Edmondson & Lei, 2014). Conversely, attempts to manufacture false certainty by overstating knowledge, overpromising timelines, or minimizing risk regularly backfire, sowing seeds of cynicism that persist long after events have stabilized.

Clear, transparent communication has been shown to calm anxiety, enhance compliance, and reduce the "interpretation gap" between teams, stakeholders, and leaders (APA, 2020; Goleman, 1995). The most trusted leaders combine honest admission of gaps or setbacks ("Here's what we still don't know") with confident articulation of action and hope ("Here's what we are doing, together"). Field studies of successful disaster responses in Scandinavia and East Asia have highlighted that cultures of transparency are correlated with higher morale, faster error reporting, and a greater willingness among all levels to speak up about red flags or other concerns, thereby reducing the risk of avoidable catastrophe (Drury, 2018; Edmondson, 2019).

Failed transparency, by contrast, often marks the beginning of institutional decline and failed leadership. The loss of trust among staff, splintered compliance from the public, and the rise of alternative information sources, credible or otherwise, quickly dominate the landscape (Phillips Kaiser, 2024). In today's environment, the ubiquity of social media accelerates this effect, amplifying both rumors and legitimate concerns at unprecedented speed.

Trust and Crisis Communication: Merkel's Example

The response to Europe's refugee crisis by Angela Merkel in 2015 stands as a lodestar of credible, trust-building crisis leadership. As the migration surge hit Germany, Merkel faced deep uncertainty, rapidly polarizing public opinion, and unprecedented pressure from all sides. Instead of offering simplistic reassurances or bowing to fear-driven demands, Merkel opted for transparent, morally anchored communication. "Wir schaffen das" – "We can do this" – became a national refrain not through bravado, but through a repeated emphasis on shared responsibility and frank admission of difficulty (PBS, 2016; The Guardian, 2015).

Merkel was explicit about the magnitude and risks, acknowledging the emotional realities faced by both refugees and citizens. "I want us to be a country where we respect every human. But I also know people are anxious. We are dealing with uncertainty" (PBS, 2016). In interviews and nationally televised addresses, Merkel was steadfast and consistent. She refused to offer cheap certainties, instead providing clear explanations of constraints, plans, and values, while demonstrating patience with public questions and dissent.

Her authenticity was supported by her visible collaboration with local leaders and civil society, as well as her consistent physical and digital presence at critical junctures. Over time, Merkel's approach not only stabilized German society during the immediate crisis but also raised global expectations for transparency, ethical clarity, and emotional honesty in leadership (APA, 2020; Edmondson, 2019).

Trust as Social Capital in Recovery and Adaptation

Longitudinal studies of post-crisis recovery underscore the enduring impact of trust on community resilience and organizational renewal. Trust creates "social capital."

In 2012, Hurricane Sandy revealed deep vulnerabilities in New York City's infrastructure, particularly its subway system, power grid, and coastal defenses. Researchers noted that the storm became a turning point for integrating climate adaptation into urban planning, thus leading to initiatives such as *Rebuild by Design* and the *Special Initiative for Rebuilding and Resiliency*. Rosenzweig and Solecki (2014) emphasized that Sandy transformed resilience from a theoretical policy concept into a practical framework for long-term city planning.

Hurricane Katrina devastated New Orleans in 2005, displacing hundreds of thousands of residents and exposing severe inequalities in housing, income, and access to emergency services. Research by Elliott and Pais (2006) found that race and socioeconomic status significantly shaped patterns of evacuation, loss, and recovery, revealing how social vulnerability amplifies disaster impact. Similarly, Abramson et al. (2015) showed that communities with greater access to social networks and resources recovered much more rapidly after displacement.

In the wake of the 2008 financial crash, the restoration of trust in public institutions was directly linked to a return of public confidence and eventual economic rebound. Networks of belief, reciprocity, and previously earned goodwill allow for faster adaptation, resource sharing, and collective healing (Edmondson, 2019; Pennebaker & Harber, 1993).

Trust and credibility are not static, they must be cultivated daily by actions, consistency, and readiness to correct course when mistakes occur (CCL, 2025; Goleman, 1995). Even considering the disparities of the response, survivors of Hurricane Katrina reported profound differences in trust levels and recovery outcomes based on the continuity and transparency of local and federal leaders. Those who were visible, remained accessible, and updated their communities honestly throughout the chaos, laid a solid foundation for steady, long-term rebuilding (Drury, 2018). Conversely, leaders who were absent, inconsistent, or opaque deepened uncertainty, hampered coordination, and left lasting scars on both institutional credibility and community resilience.

Credibility, in the end, is not guaranteed by title or office, but generated by a repeated pattern of honesty, openness, respect, and genuine emotional engagement before, during, and after the physical and emotional storm.

Case Integration: Hard Lessons in Building and Losing Trust

The 2015 refugee crisis in Europe placed Angela Merkel and Germany on the world stage, where trust was both tested and rebuilt. When masses of people crossed the continent seeking safety, Merkel resisted both populist calls for immediate closure and simplistic optimism. Instead, she acknowledged the gravity of the challenge and her own uncertainty, while committing to upholding Germany's constitutional values and providing pragmatic support to both newcomers and established citizens alike (PBS, 2016). Merkel's willingness to communicate consistently, stand tall in the face of boisterous criticism, and respond to shifting realities nurtured a durable, though sometimes hard-won, resilience within German society and the European Union (APA, 2020; The Guardian, 2015).

Contrast this with well-documented cases where opacity and false certainty have destroyed trust. During the Chernobyl nuclear disaster of 1986, Soviet authorities issued contradictory statements and withheld information from first responders, citizens, and even partner governments. This deliberate lack of transparency had decades-long consequences for institutional legitimacy in the region and fostered a culture of rumor and skepticism that remains evident today (Drury, 2018; Edmondson, 2019).

Within organizations, companies like Johnson & Johnson (J&J), whose Tylenol recall is still studied as a gold standard, preempted the loss of credibility by over-communicating risks, decisions, and changes, pairing honest updates with visible action and sustained emotional engagement (Goleman, 1995; Pennebaker & Harber, 1993).

In each case above, the thread is clear. Trust is built by the leader who is present, joining their people in uncertainty and shared vulnerability, modeling transparency and care with unwavering consistency, even when initial events create confusion, uncertainty, and doubt.

Leadership Toolbox: The Practice and Repair of Trust

Purpose: To equip leaders and organizations with practical tools for building, sustaining, and, when needed, restoring trust and credibility through crisis.

- **Active Consistency Checklist:** Deliver on every promise made, no matter how small. Publicly track progress and openly explain setbacks, acknowledging the successes, even the small ones.

- **Explicit Social Proof:** Visibly follow all instructions, safety measures, and the policies of specialized agencies or authorities before asking others on your team and in your community to do the same. Leverage early adopters and positive outliers as peer exemplars.

- **Transparency Protocols:** Communicate uncertainties and risks with clear "what we know/what we don't/what we're doing" statements. When information changes, explain why and how it changes.

- **Authority Humility Pairing:** Pair factual expertise with model vulnerability, be the first to say, "I don't have all the answers," and then facilitate community problem-solving and adaptation.

- **Feedback Channels:** Maintain open and available paths for public and team feedback, including town halls, anonymous reporting opportunities, and digital Q&A, and acknowledge what is heard with visible adjustments.

- **Rumor Audit:** Routinely scan for rumors and misinformation, mobilize respected figures to counter with factual, empathetic correction.

- **After-Action Trust Reviews:** Following every critical period, conduct a trust debrief. What built confidence? What lost it? Where did social proof and transparency succeed or fail?

Repair Rituals: If trust is broken, address it head-on. Publicly admit errors, update on lessons learned, and outline concrete next steps for realignment.

One of the most essential elements of this phase is accurately tracking the information being disseminated, thereby providing a constant opportunity to update the community on progress and identify areas that are proving problematic. This will further cement trust and credibility while garnering community support and involvement toward building solutions.

7. COGNITIVE FLEXIBILITY AND ADAPTION

Tunnel Vision vs. Wide-Angle Awareness under Stress

Crises exert a powerful gravitational force on individual and collective perception. Acute stress is notorious for driving "tunnel vision," a narrowing of awareness that restricts decision-making fields and encourages a stubborn reliance on habit, routine, or the salience of immediate threats (Grupe & Nitschke, 2013; SHRM, 2025). While this instinct shields against overwhelming information, it leaves organizations vulnerable to hidden risks, strategic blind spots, and the loss of alternative options.

For groups required to make sense of rapidly changing, dynamic situations, unmitigated tunnel vision can lead to catastrophic errors or missed opportunities. These misses might range from logistics failures in emergency supply chains to dangerous escalations in crowd management (Brandfolder, 2023; Drury, 2018). The first step is being aware that tunnel vision can and does happen!

Cognitive flexibility, by contrast, is the disciplined act of stretching one's "field of view," continuously shifting between focused execution and broad situational scanning (LeadingSapiens, 2025). In the 2010 Chilean mine rescue, this skill was evident as engineers alternated between relentless drilling and open innovation, mobilizing public, private, and scientific input to solve for pathways through and around unprecedented barriers (Brandfolder, 2023). Elite military and disaster teams train "wide-

67

angle awareness" by rotating commanders, requiring rapid environmental sense-making, and embedding "spotters" who are accountable for pattern recognition at the system's edges (Drury, 2018; SHRM, 2025).

Leaders with mature cognitive flexibility recognize that effective crisis response involves continually toggling between micro and macro focus, balancing the pressure to execute with relentless curiosity and adaptation. These leaders foster an environment where pausing to "scan the horizon" is not only permitted but expected. When inquiry, not just action, is rewarded, and where innovative cross-talk directly counterbalances stress's innate narrowing effects, solutions present themselves (Edmondson, 2019; Risk & Resilience Hub, 2025).

Divergent Thinking in Problem-Solving

Adaptive problem-solving is fundamentally a practice in divergent thinking, actively generating possibilities, entertaining unconventional strategies, and exploring parallel paths to solution (Brandfolder, 2023; Edmondson, 2019). Crises, due to their non-linear and volatile nature, require an increased tolerance for ambiguity and iterative exploration. Diverse teams excel under these conditions, as their different backgrounds and mental models prompt broader searches and more comprehensive scenario mapping (Doodle, 2025; Fiveable, 2024).

Divergent thinking was crucial during the height of the COVID-19 pandemic as hospital systems, logistics planners, and policymakers swapped traditional protocols for real-time experimentation. In New York's overtaxed hospitals, for example, physician and nurse teams conducted daily "option bursts" in which rapid-fire, 90-second pitches for new workflows were tested and the best advanced to the next cycle (Doodle, 2025). The result? Innovations in PPE reuse, care team rotation, and patient flow that fundamentally reshaped national best practice.

Great leaders actively structure their organizations for divergent thinking. They introduce scenario-planning boot camps, appoint rotating "devil's advocates," and systematically pair top-down command with bottom-up innovation (Brandfolder, 2023; SHRM, 2025). Whether through red teaming in military units, hackathons in tech firms, or "tiger teams" in manufacturing, the effort to build in cognitive friction consistently delivers better solutions under pressure.

How Great Leaders Encourage Adaptive Teams

Creating teams that pivot effortlessly in chaos requires more than charisma, it demands intentional cultivation of climates where cognitive experimentation, dissent, and learning flourish (Edmondson, 2019; Highrise, 2023). Leader openness to new perspectives, regardless of source, is the backbone of agility. This openness is built on several key behaviors, including

- Inviting junior and marginalized voices to daylight challenges and risks, then acting rapidly on credible insights.

- De-stigmatizing error and failure, allocating scheduled reflection time for learning from surprise, not just success.

- Blending structure (protocols, checklists) with open-reflection interludes, ensuring adaptation rather than mere adherence (Edmondson, 2019; SHRM, 2025).

- Assigning rotating roles such as scouts for blind spots, scenario builders, and risk auditors to keep organizational inertia at bay.

- Practicing "non-stationarity" by explicitly acknowledging and planning for the idea that the crisis environment is constantly changing, requiring constant refresh (Ambrose, 1994; LeadingSapiens, 2025).

The build-up to the D-Day landings in 1944 provides the quintessential template.

Eisenhower refused to follow a single path or adopt a uniform doctrine, instead guiding hundreds of planners through "what if" drills, requiring robust dissent at every level, and assigning full authority for local improvisation in the field. As dozens of variables, such as weather, enemy movement, and logistics, shifted hour by hour, this distributed, adaptive command structure enabled the Allies not only to invade under the worst conditions but also to improvise and recover at every turn (Ambrose, 1994).

Case Integration: Eisenhower and D-Day's Multi-Level Adaption

Dwight Eisenhower's stewardship of *Operation Overlord* stands as a masterclass in operational and cognitive flexibility. Rather than anchoring to any static battle script, Eisenhower worked with his commanders on vast webs of contingency plans, iterating through simulations for nearly every conceivable failure, including tide tables gone awry, adverse weather conditions, incorrect intelligence, or leadership casualties (Ambrose, 1994).

In the pivotal 48 hours before the Normandy landings, weather data shifted dramatically. Eisenhower's process was notable. Rather than dictating unilateral direction, he led searching debates, solicited dissent from junior officers, and ultimately made the call to proceed, demonstrating both confidence and adaptive humility. Field commanders, already authorized to pivot off-plan, unleashed new tactics as conditions evolved, and the distributed response outperformed even the most carefully written plans (Ambrose, 1994).

Eisenhower's blend of preparation, cognitive diversity, and faith in subordinate innovation proved vital. The D-Day experience cemented the imperative for future crisis leaders. In the face of complexity and volatility, decisive vision must be paired with an unerring trust in your people, at every rank, and in the ability to course-correct at every level. Wide-angle thinking, divergent action, and local adaptation together form the true backbone of victory under pressure (Edmondson, 2019; Risk & Resilience Hub, 2025).

Leadership Toolbox: Cognitive Flexibility in Action

Purpose: To give leaders concrete methods for building, broadening, and sustaining cognitive flexibility and adaptive problem-solving capacity in crisis teams.

- **Rotating Perspective Routines:** Implement regular meetings where team members must pitch, critique, and defend opposing solutions, and reward the team member who provides the broadest situational insights.

- **Scenario Sprint Labs:** Lead fast-paced exercises in which teams draft parallel "what if" plans, stress-test assumptions, and gamify reacting to shifting constraints.

- **Resilience Debriefs:** Reserve time after every phase or incident to ask, "What did we miss? What surprised us? What must we question next?"

- **Local Adaptation Mandate:** Establish explicit boundaries for when the protocol can be adapted or procedurally overridden, empowering frontline improvisation.

  Frontline commanders, regardless of title or rank, must feel empowered and supported by senior leadership, encouraging them to make decisive, situational judgments with confidence, knowing that initiative in the field will be trusted, not punished.

- **Blindspot Scouts:** Assign rotating individuals to spot neglected or shifting risks, ensuring new data and voices get attention in the "noise" of crisis flow.

- **Learning Journals and Surprise Logs:** Encourage teams to log moments and document where initial assumptions were incorrect and identify the triggers for necessary pivots.

- **Feedback Amplification:** Build multiple, redundant channels for field feedback, and publicly celebrate fast, effective course corrections and unexpected wins.

8. MODELING RESILIENCE

Social Learning Theory and Role-Model Behaviors

In every crisis, people look to leaders not just for direction, but for emotional cues and behavioral templates. Social learning theory, rooted in the work of Albert Bandura, posits that individuals learn new behaviors, attitudes, and coping strategies by observing those around them, especially those they regard as credible, similar, or aspirational (Bandura, 1977; SimplyPsychology, 2025). In traumatic or uncertain environments, the effect is multiplied. Followers adapt not only to what leaders say but also to how they visibly respond to setbacks, perceived complexity, and the unknown (DTIC, 2023; Emerald, 2024). Organizations that foster resilience acknowledge this by designing leadership training, internal communications protocols, and peer mentoring to ensure that adaptive behaviors are consistently modeled at every level (Agile Group, 2025).

Repeated research across the U.S. military, emergency medicine, and education has consistently demonstrated that the presence of resilient role models enhances the group's collective ability to recover from adversity (Gu, Q., & Day, C., 2007; Robertson, H. D., Elliott, A. M., Burton, C., Iversen, L., Murchie, P., Porteous, T., & Matheson, C., 2016; Southwick, S. M., Bonanno, G. A., Masten, A. S., Panter-Brick, C., & Yehuda, R., 2014). This link is mediated by the sense of belonging and shared purpose that emerges when followers recognize themselves in their leaders, whether through similar backgrounds, shared experiences, or articulated values (Drury, 2018; DTIC, 2023). At the heart of resilient teams and societies are

73

visible exemplars, whose persistent optimism, adaptive coping, and calm in adversity nudge others toward hope and collective action.

Visible Coping Strategies Leaders Can Display

Beyond words, visible coping strategies form the organizational language of resilience. Leaders who demonstrate concrete behaviors such as accepting uncertainty, seeking assistance, showing vulnerability, and recovering quickly from setbacks create a culture in which these acts are both possible and expected (Edmondson, 2019; Goleman, 1995). Role modeling encompasses not just "power poses" but also the open display of regulatory techniques, such as pausing to slow down and breathe in stressful meetings, asking for feedback in real-time, or initiating group gratitude moments (Manz & Neck, 2004). Recognition of subordinates provides motivation, reinforces desired behaviors, and strengthens organizational cohesion.

Self-leadership literature also highlights strategies such as positive self-talk and affirmations, deliberate self-reflection, and visualization of successful outcomes, all of which can be made explicit in group or public settings (Edmondson, 2019; Emerald, 2024). Visible coping inspires collective resilience through both explicit imitation ("If my leader tries, so can I") and implicit permission ("It's acceptable here to acknowledge fear but move forward anyway") (Emerald, 2024).

In 2017, Puerto Rico was battered by massive hurricanes. While landfall occurred in September 2017, violent storms persisted through the early part of 2018, resulting in more than 3,000 souls lost (some studies cite more than 4,000 souls lost). During this period, municipal leaders who demonstrated tenacity and took visible steps to care for their own families and then communicated "we are in this together" shaped community choices and morale far more than those who retreated or projected false bravado (Highrise, 2023). Resilience is thus contagious, spread by demonstration rather than edict (Emerald, 2024).

Psychology of Hope and Solution Focus

Resilience flourishes in the soil of hope, fed by a solution-focused mindset. Hope in psychology is defined not as blind optimism, but as the belief that meaningful action is possible, even in the face of adversity (PositivePsychology, 2025; Snyder, 1991). Successful crisis leaders are those who project a solution-focused thinking model that setbacks are not endpoints, but merely data that provides the impetus for adjustment and innovation (Edmondson, 2019). This is visible in leaders who ask, "What now?" after a loss, who celebrate incremental progress, and who foreground agency over circumstance.

Hopeful, action-oriented thinking buffers individuals and systems from the effects of learned helplessness, a danger in prolonged, drawn-out, or highly traumatic crises (Bandura, 1995). Science and experience alike show that teams and communities that are engaged with frequent reminders of progress and invited to participate in co-creating solutions demonstrate greater motivation, perseverance, and creativity. This style of leadership is not naïve, it acknowledges the harsh realities of the situation but insists on the group's capacity to adapt (Drury, 2018; Edmondson, 2019).

Resilient Role Modeling in Action: The Zelensky Example

President Volodymyr Zelensky's leadership during the 2022 Russian invasion of Ukraine offers a contemporary masterclass in modeling resilience for national and global audiences. Rather than hiding or delegating difficult moments, Zelensky remained in Kyiv, broadcasting regular video updates that depicted him walking through government buildings, meeting with aides, and joining front-line defenders (BBC, 2022). These visible behaviors, showing presence under direct threat, accepting uncertainty ("The outcome is not clear, but we persist"), and framing the crisis as a quest for national dignity, became touchstones of hope and defiance. As a result, not only Ukrainian resistance but global support was engendered (NYT, 2022).

Crucially, Zelensky's approach fused vulnerability ("We are afraid; we don't know what tomorrow brings") with agency ("We fight together; we will rebuild"). The result? Authenticity. His daily communications revealed both grief and determination. At the same time, small gestures such as declining rescue for himself while advocating for the care of civilians signaled a standard of sacrifice and collective identity (BBC, 2022; NYT, 2022). Military, business, and nonprofit leaders worldwide continue to cite his example in their efforts toward cultivating hope, courage, and moral clarity among their own teams (PositivePsychology, 2025).

Case Integration: Role Models, Belonging, and Societal Resilience

Throughout history and in every sector, resilient leaders have rewritten the probabilities of survival and growth by functioning as living proof that hope and adaptation are always possible. Following September 11, 2001, New York's daily press briefings featured not just technical updates but also repeated endorsements of visible coping activities, such as walking through neighborhoods, comforting the bereaved, and hosting spiritual and community rituals. These moments combined expertise and empathy, embedding authentic resilience into the city's recovery narrative (Edmondson, 2019).

In global business, leaders at firms recovering from shock layoffs or market upheaval have adopted "visible resilience rounds," moving through teams to candidly discuss challenges, narrate small wins, and acknowledge emotions. These acts translate high-level strategy into daily, lived experience, reinforcing the tenets of social learning theory and increasing both loyalty and performance (Agile Group, 2025).

The most adaptive organizations recognize that role modeling is not an abstract ideal but a daily, operational necessity. It shapes choices, transforms emotion, and builds the patterns of collective hope that make recovery reproducible (Bandura, 1977; Drury, 2018; Edmondson, 2019; Emerald, 2024).

Leadership Toolbox: Leading with Resilience

Purpose: To provide a practical suite for leaders seeking to cultivate personal and collective resilience through role modeling, explicit coping, and the reinforcement of hope.

- **Visible Coping Templates:** Regularly and authentically demonstrate intentional stress management. Use visible self-regulation, narrate personal setbacks and recoveries, and invite others to do the same.

- **Social Learning Rituals:** Create recurring team rituals, such as shared gratitude, debriefs, and progress celebrations, to normalize visible resilience and mutual inspiration.

- **Model Belonging:** Actively connect with different subgroups, share your own learning process, and invite mentorship connections between experienced and newer team members.

- **Narrate the Solution Journey:** When addressing setbacks, lead with "Here's how we adapted," focusing on process as much as outcome.

- **Hope Boards and Feedback Loops:** Feature visual progress displays and public forums for celebrating micro-wins, surfacing new solutions, and inviting open problem-solving.

- **Daily Modeling Feedback:** Invite colleagues to share where they have observed resilience in themselves, their peers, leaders (especially those whom they admire), or other team members, thereby building a living bank of examples.

- **Vulnerability Pairing:** Share your own struggles constructively, modeling acceptance and positive orientation toward change.

- **Role Model Audits:** Periodically survey teams to identify whose behaviors are inspiring and create opportunities to amplify their influence across the organization.

PART II

Leadership in Action
Real World Crisis

9. NATURAL DISASTERS

Hurricane Katrina (2005): Breakdowns in Leadership

The devastation wrought by Hurricane Katrina in 2005 remains one of the starkest illustrations of the perils of fractured crisis leadership. Despite advance warnings and decades of scenario planning, the disaster response was marred by confusion, delayed decision-making, and a lack of true command presence at every level of government (Cato Institute, 2025; Drury, 2018; Martinko, Gundlach, & Douglas, 2009). Authority bias, ordinarily a group strength, became a liability, as citizens, first responders, and even outside aid providers waited for direction while public officials hesitated, pointed fingers, or communicated contradictory orders (Cato Institute, 2025).

Leadership failures cascaded. The federal government, state officials, and local leaders, such as New Orleans' Mayor Ray Nagin, exhibited poor preparation, deflected responsibility, and failed to coordinate essential resources (ShareOK, 2024; Wikipedia, 2005). Crisis communication vacillated as evacuation orders were delayed, plans for the city's most vulnerable were incomplete, and leaders sometimes prioritized blame-shifting or optics over substance of the message. These breakdowns eroded public trust and left communities adrift, fueling rumors, panic, and more loss of life. Key reports condemned Katrina as "a litany of mistakes, misjudgments, lapses, and absurdities all cascading together, blinding us to what was coming and hobbling any collective effort to respond...across the core of the government response" (Martinko et al., 2009; ShareOK, 2024; Wikipedia, 2005).

The result was an erosion of social trust, the rise of rumor, and a devastating sense of abandonment among the most vulnerable. Social proof failed as public and emergency responders alike found few credible models for coping, adaptation, or hope (Drury, 2018). In the chaos, survivors and grassroots leaders sometimes stepped into the leadership vacuum, an enduring reminder that resilience can emerge from below – from anywhere – when institutional trust falters.

Fukushima Earthquake/Tsunami (2011): Proactive Japanese Crisis Communication

The Fukushima Daiichi nuclear disaster in 2011 is generally considered a mixed but largely cautionary example of the psychology of crisis leadership, depending on which aspects you examine. Fukushima illustrates the consequences of poor crisis leadership at the very top: delayed communication, rigid protocols, and suppressed dissent, resulting in eroded trust and slowed response. In contrast to Hurricane Katrina, at the same time, improvised solutions by independent teams on the front lines and from Tokyo Electric Power Company (TEPCO) itself, highlight the critical role of agency and adaptability. When all the facts are considered in aggregate, the case underscores the verity that transparency, rapid decision-making, and empowering frontline actors are essential components towards the successful management of high-stakes crises.

The 2011 Fukushima earthquake, tsunami, and nuclear disaster in Japan revealed both the challenges and advances of proactive crisis management. Despite the catastrophic scale – three reactors melting down, massive infrastructure destruction, and over 150,000 evacuees – key aspects of the immediate Japanese response, primarily at the local level, were defined by transparency, coordinated messaging, and a concerted effort to sustain trust amid overwhelming uncertainty (IAEA, 2015; Sasakawa Peace Foundation, 2024; World Nuclear Association, 2024).

While Japan's initial management of the crisis was hampered by destroyed communication systems and thus, a need to improvise emergency plans, central leaders and agencies rapidly moved to acknowledge what was known and what was not. As social proof emerged and grew among responding entities, repeated updates, consistent use of scientific experts, delaying the assignment of blame, and openness to international assistance reflected a marked shift from the management failures of past global disasters (Fukushima Investigation Committee, 2012; IAEA, 2015). Both local governments and TEPCO, although later criticized for certain omissions, sought to establish live press briefings and direct lines of communication to evacuees, conveying both the challenges and progress in stabilization efforts (Sasakawa Peace Foundation, 2024; Wikipedia, 2011).

Unlike Katrina, where credibility and public confidence dissolved, Japan's rapid adaption and subsequent visible blend of transparency and humility enabled many communities to absorb the shock and collaborate on evacuation, containment, and later, on recovery initiatives. Networks of neighborhood volunteers, frequent digital and on-site updates, and the willingness of officials to say, "We are unsure, but this is what we are doing together," provided new social anchors, nurtured psychological resilience, and facilitated collective learning under the grimmest conditions (Drury, 2018; IAEA, 2015).

Case Integration: Lessons from Two Disasters

Hurricane Katrina and the Fukushima response remain two important object lessons in the social psychology of disaster. In New Orleans, the absence of authentic, coordinated leadership and the resulting communication vacuum allowed fear and confusion to metastasize, proving that technical competence alone cannot overcome a lack of public trust and credible models of resilience (Drury, 2018; Martinko et al., 2009; Wikipedia, 2005). By contrast, Japan's crisis leaders, even as they initially struggled with the early response and some early communications, ultimately demonstrated transparency, acknowledged uncertainty, and worked to integrate community-based problem-solving as the disaster unfolded (Fukushima Investigation Committee, 2012; IAEA, 2015).

These examples underscore the essential, non-technical elements of successful disaster response including visible role models, credible transparency, emotional acknowledgment, and the sustained reinforcement of social patterns that channel distress into hope, obstruction into cooperation, and inflexible behavior and confusion into adaptive action (Drury, 2018; Edmondson, 2019).

Leadership Toolbox: Resilience in Natural Disaster Leadership

Purpose: To equip leaders and agencies with actionable strategies for visible crisis modeling, rapid communication, and collective resilience during natural disasters.

- **Anchor in Visibility:** Leaders should remain physically and digitally present, routinely update their presence, and tangibly engage with the affected community.

- **Admit and Communicate Uncertainty:** Share what is unknown as openly as what is known, and explain what steps are underway to clarify or control risk, even if you don't have all the information.

- **Activate Social Models:** Elevate grassroots leaders, survivors, and volunteers as peer role models, spotlight acts of visible coping and hope.

- **Establish Recovery Feedback Loops:** Build mechanisms for public input and reaction, use them to inform subsequent actions and updates.

- **Empower Decentralized Response:** Enable local adaptation and community-driven planning in zones where central direction cannot reach or is overwhelmed.

- **Regular Public Briefings:** Maintain daily or frequent information cycles, allowing for Q&A and encouraging direct questions, even in emotionally charged or high-stress settings.

- **Debrief for Growth:** Once the acute crisis passes, systematize learning reviews, maintain transparency about what failed and what succeeded, and update plans, protocols, and messaging, including your safety binder, based on those lessons for the future.

10. PUBLIC HEALTH EMERGENCIES

COVID-19 Pandemic Global Contrasts: Leadership and Messaging

The COVID-19 pandemic presented the ultimate global stress test for leadership styles, crisis communication, and public trust. In the early months of 2020, different nations revealed striking contrasts in the clarity, authority, and empathy of their responses, contrasts which often correlated with both health outcomes and social cohesion (PMC, 2023; Van Bavel et al., 2020). Assertive, science-based leadership and disciplined, consistent messaging allowed some societies to rally rapidly, while confusion and contradictory signals left others exposed to both viral and psychological contagion (Harvard Kennedy School, 2022; The Forge, 2025; Wikipedia, 2021).

Social learning theory was at work on a population scale. When leaders modeled evidence-based behaviors such as washing hands, wearing masks, and restricting movement, groups learned and accepted new norms, then adapted accordingly (Bandura, 1977; Drury, 2018). When public figures squabbled, denied problems, or delivered conflicting advice, social proof deteriorated. Rumor and divisiveness filled the vacuum. The difference between a united national response and social fragmentation was rarely, if ever, determined solely by technical capacity, but by the credibility, consistency, and emotional resonance of communication (Frontiers in Public Health, 2024; Van Bavel et al., 2020).

New Zealand: Assertive Leadership and Consistency

New Zealand, under Prime Minister Jacinda Ardern, became an international exemplar of clear, empathetic crisis leadership. From the outset, Ardern's team acted early and decisively by closing borders, communicating public health rules in simple and accessible language, and visibly embracing expert guidance (CompCoRe, 2021; The Forge, 2025). Her regular TV and social media briefings were deeply human. She openly acknowledged anxiety by explaining hard choices, and reinforcing "team of five million" identity cues (Doodle, 2025).

Crucially, Ardern demonstrated the behaviors she prescribed, proactively modeling mask use, public distancing and, when necessary, government transparency about changing science and policies (Van Bavel et al., 2020). Citizens saw their national story reframed as one of collective responsibility and hope. Psychological safety was supported by daily COVID-19 updates, an emphasis on kindness, and explicit permission to mourn setbacks while adapting (Drury, 2018; Edmondson, 2019). Effective governance and a lack of partisan infighting created reinforcing cycles of trust, compliance, and resilience (Doodle, 2025; PMC, 2023).

Brazil and U.S.: Inconsistent Messaging, Fragmentation, and Distrust

By contrast, responses in countries such as Brazil and the United States were characterized by inconsistent messaging and weak, politicized science leadership in the critical early months (Frontiers in Public Health, 2024; The Forge, 2025; Van Bavel et al., 2020). Federal leaders in both nations initially minimized risks, contradicted health advisors, or shifted blame, resulting in public confusion and divergent rules at state and local levels (CompCoRe, 2021; Harvard Kennedy School, 2022).

In the U.S., the lack of sustained, visible modeling of protective behavior by key officials undermined the social learning process, while contradictory state and federal guidance fractured public trust (Harvard Kennedy School, 2022; PMC, 2023). In Brazil, President Jair Bolsonaro dismissed the virus as a "little flu," openly broke quarantine restrictions, and publicly disparaged both scientists and political rivals, discouraging coordinated public response (Frontiers in Public Health, 2024). Social identity theory and group psychology predict precisely this outcome: in the absence of trusted role models and consensus signals, populations default to subgroup loyalty, mistrust authority, and perpetuate division (Drury, 2018).

Case Integration: Social Proof and the Cost of Mixed Signals

New Zealand's case remains a powerful demonstration of the mechanics of social learning and resilience. When Ardern said, "Stay home to save lives" and modeled those behaviors day after day, public compliance and emotional well-being remained strong even during prolonged lockdowns. Mistakes and setbacks were acknowledged and corrected, reframing them as shared learning opportunities rather than failures (Doodle, 2025; Edmondson, 2019). This climate of trust and teamwork not only flattened the initial curve but enabled people to recover faster, both psychologically and economically.

By contrast, the inconsistent, politicized, and unscientific tone of early U.S. and Brazilian responses led to waves of misinformation, persistent anxiety, and public resistance to the most basic health measures (PMC, 2023; Van Bavel et al., 2020). In the absence of unified modeling, rumors flourished. When mask mandates were issued, many in the population viewed them as partisan attacks rather than acts of public solidarity. The pandemic's psychological and physical toll was amplified by this breakdown in credible modeling and a lack of shared identity.

What these divergent cases reveal is that in public health emergencies, effective leadership is less about charisma or even resources than about modeling trust, prioritizing consistency, and visibly aligning with the behaviors required for community adaptation and survival (Bandura, 1977; Frontiers in Public Health, 2024; The Forge, 2025).

Leadership Toolbox: Modeling Public Health Resilience

Purpose: To enable leaders and institutions to model, reinforce, and sustain public resilience and behavioral adaptation during extended health crises.

- **Unified Communication Protocols:** Pre-align language, science messaging, and visible behaviors across all layers of leadership before major announcements. Consistency is key!

- **Expert Visibility:** Regularly feature and empower scientists and public health leaders in decision-making and communications. Leaders model heedfulness by visibly deferring to authentic expertise.

- **Transparent Adaptation:** Incorporate transparent, public learning cycles for new data, admit when guidance changes, explain why, and demonstrate humility.

   Remember! Empathy enhances social identity and, in crisis situations, will always prevail over command-and-control strategies.

- **Behavioral Modeling Campaigns:** Develop public rituals, symbols, and media campaigns that make required behaviors (such as masking and distancing) visible, normalized, and identity-building.

- **Community-Owned Narratives:** Amplify stories of resilience, adaptation, and local solution-finding from diverse voices, and elevate community champions.

- **Feedback Infrastructures:** Maintain open feedback portals, hotlines, and Q&A sessions to surface confusion, rumor, and new barriers, with prompt, empathetic response cycles.

- **Role Model Networks:** Identify and equip community, religious, and business leaders to consistently display new norms and allow this to extend modeling beyond government.

- **Adaptive Policy Review:** After each public health phase, systematically debrief, audit, and iterate both the messaging and the behaviors expected of all leadership strata.

11. POLITICAL AND SECURITY SHOCKS

September 11, 2001: Rudy Giuliani as Symbolic Presence

The morning of September 11, 2001, catapulted New York City – and the world – into an unprecedented crisis of fear, uncertainty, and loss. As the twin towers fell and chaos rippled through Manhattan, Mayor Rudy Giuliani emerged as the city's symbolic anchor. His presence provided visible, consistent, and emotionally resonant leadership that transcended political and social divides (Drury, 2018; NYT, 2007). Giuliani's leadership in those hours was rooted not in technical expertise, but in mastery of psychological visibility and message discipline. He walked the streets, appeared at press briefings, and communicated with both confidence and vulnerability, giving a voice to the city's collective shock while reinforcing the need to hold together (Army.mil, 2012).

Giuliani's presence provided a template for coping that citizens, both in New York and beyond, could emulate (Bandura, 1977). Through clear, repeated messaging, a willingness to be seen grieving and directing, and the embodiment of unflinching civility and resolve, Giuliani promoted social proof and unity. The simplicity of his instructions ("Stay calm. Help each other. We will continue") created a baseline for behavior that preempted mass panic and encouraged pro-social adaptation (Drury, 2018; JBA, 2009). The resulting wave of volunteerism and resilience was not solely the product of organizational capacity, but of visible, psychologically intelligent modeling in the eye of national trauma.

Yet Giuliani's symbolic role was not without limits or controversy. Criticisms in subsequent years have focused on gaps in preparation, public health communication, and uneven access to support for vulnerable populations (NYT, 2007). Still, on the day itself, and in the days that followed, his capacity to unify, give meaning, and model recovery offers a vivid example of the enduring power of psychological presence in a security crisis.

Oslo Terror Attack, 2011: Jens Stoltenberg's Unifying Calm

Nearly a decade later, on July 22, 2011, Norway faced its own shock when a far-right-wing terrorist slaughtered 77 souls in bombings and mass shootings against the government, the civilian population, and at a Workers' Youth League summer camp. In the aftermath, Prime Minister Jens Stoltenberg gathered a grieving nation before him, appearing on national broadcasts, attending memorials, and speaking to both the bereaved and the world in carefully chosen, steadied tones. Unlike Giuliani's kinetic visibility, Stoltenberg's unifying calm was expressed through language from the Norwegian cultural tradition as he proclaimed, "Our answer shall be more democracy, more openness, and more humanity" (Stoltenberg, as cited in BBC, 2011).

Stoltenberg's behavior reflected the insight of social learning theory, that followers not only copy behaviors but also the emotional register and value frames set by leaders (Bandura, 1977; Drury, 2018). By actively rejecting calls for retribution or an authoritarian crackdown, and visibly sharing in national mourning, Stoltenberg reinforced pro-social norms, countering fear with collective identity and hope (BBC, 2011). Repeated surveys found that Norwegians across generations identified closely with his example of making space to grieve, while also recognizing the importance of creative recovery rituals, open gatherings, flower marches, and spontaneous commemoration within communities.

His response was widely credited with reducing the risk of social division, revenge, or policy overreaction. Simultaneously, fostering a culture of inclusive resilience. Stoltenberg's transparency ("We do not have all the answers, but we face them together") and continued public engagement helped preserve psychological safety at a moment when polarization and distrust could have easily flourished (Drury, 2018).

Case Integration: Visible Role-Modeling Under Shock

Both 9-11 in New York and the Oslo terror attacks reveal how the immediate presence, composure, and communication of political leaders shape the foundation for societal adaptation. Giuliani's wading into the dust and crowds of Manhattan provided a real-time, shared blueprint for endurance and recovery, his simple guidance threading hope through overwhelming horror (Drury, 2018; NYT, 2007). Stoltenberg, for his part, offered a vision of national cohesion and dignity that explicitly resisted the psychology of vengeance, inviting imitation in communities large and small (BBC, 2011).

The contrasts and parallels between these two moments highlight key mechanisms of resilience, including Leaders as the embodiment of group norms, the deliberate modeling of visible coping, and the crafting of identity through both words and presence. Both men's approaches, although differing in tone and tempo, validated public emotions, established psychological anchors, and amplified the collective capacity for meaning-making. In doing so, they serve as powerful models for crisis leadership in the modern security environment.

Leadership Toolbox: Adaptive Political Presence in Crisis

Purpose: To provide leaders facing security or political shocks with actionable strategies for harnessing symbolic presence, emotional clarity, and pro-social recovery.

- **Visible Anchor Protocol:** Prioritize physical and broadcast visibility; leaders should be present in or at both sites of trauma and forums of public discussion.

- **Emotionally Synchronous Messaging:** Acknowledge fear and grief directly, but pair with calm, hope, and core identity messages, repeating central themes.

"We don't have all the answers or yet understand why this happened, but we will. We have some of the most experienced and qualified people in the country working on those answers right now, and we will share them with you as soon as we can."

- **Behavioral Modeling:** Demonstrate desired coping and resilience, not only through speech, but also through direct action (walking in public spaces, participating in memorials, and sustaining engagement).

- **Inclusive Identity Construction:** Utilize language and ritual to foster a shared identity, avoiding divisive or punitive rhetoric.

- **Peer and Community Amplification:** Highlight and elevate examples of grassroots unity, local leaders, and ordinary citizens enacting pro-social adaptation.

- **Feedback and Ritual Review:** Enable public reflection, dialogue, and commemoration as a standard crisis response, regularly review national or local rituals to enhance recovery.

- **Transparent Learning:** Publicly identify what is known, what remains unclear, and where adaptation is ongoing, modeling humility and fostering ongoing collective navigation.

12. ORGANIZATIONAL AND ECONOMIC CRISIS

Johnson & Johnson's Tylenol Crisis (1982): Restoring Public Trust

The Tylenol crisis of 1982 stands as a gold standard for organizational resilience and transparent leadership in the face of devastating uncertainty. When seven people in the Chicago area died after ingesting Tylenol product tainted with cyanide, Johnson & Johnson (J&J) faced a situation threatening not only a flagship product but the collective trust of millions (Greyser, 1982; PBS, 2014; Wikipedia, 2003). The stakes were immense. Tylenol represented a third of J&J's profit growth and nearly 40% of the U.S. painkiller market, with hundreds of millions of consumers at risk (Johnson & Johnson, 2015; OU, 1997).

Instead of denial or delay, J&J's leadership acted with uninhibited speed and candor. Within days, the company issued public health warnings, suspended production and advertising, and initiated a nationwide recall, pulling 31 million bottles, valued at over $100 million. This was done despite knowing that sabotage likely occurred outside their factory (PBS, 2014; Wikipedia, 2003). Senior executives appeared at press briefings, explained what was known and unknown, and emphasized consumer safety over short-term profits. Through open and honest communication with both customers and regulators, Johnson & Johnson reinforced its commitment to transparency, accountability, and public safety; therefore, laying the groundwork to rebuild trust and demonstrate integrity in the face of crisis. (Greyser, 1982; Sciencedirect, 2023).

Crucially, J&J paired transparency with visible role modeling and a solution-focused approach. Offering refunds, introducing tamper-evident packaging (redefining global industry standards), and using clear, accessible language across all platforms (OU, 1997; PBS, 2014). Their recognition that restoring trust is both behavioral and emotional, grounded in empathy, action, and accountability, changed the blueprint for crisis management. In the years that followed, Tylenol regained its lost market share, and J&J's brand became synonymous with ethical, consumer-facing leadership (Greyser, 1982; Johnson & Johnson, 2015).

Financial Leadership: Fed and U.S. Treasury During the 2008 Meltdown

The financial crisis of 2008 posed a threat not only to firms and corporations but also to the stability of the global economy. As credit dried up and core banks faltered, the U.S. Treasury and Federal Reserve faced unprecedented complexity, ambiguity, and political pressure (Ben Bernanke, 2015; HBS, 2023). Their subsequent response illustrates the core crisis leadership principles of clarity, decisive intervention, and behavioral modeling at a scale affecting billions.

Ben Bernanke (Fed) and Henry Paulson (Treasury), along with other key actors, signaled a willingness to act beyond precedent, rapidly injecting liquidity, guaranteeing deposits, and crafting emergency rescue packages for critical institutions (Bernanke, 2015; Harvard Kennedy School, 2022). Unlike actions taken during past recessions, they prioritized daily public briefings, bipartisan coordination, and clear, jargon-free explanations of actions that would otherwise have seemed technical or opaque (HBS, 2023; Wikipedia, 2023). Their communication struck a crucial balance between honesty and risk ("We face grave uncertainty, but here's what we're doing now"). In doing so, they provided a reassurance, as well as a commitment to economic recovery.

Despite controversy, these measures helped stabilize global markets and channeled collective anxiety. Social learning theory was again at play. Visible leadership, paired with unity and repeated, direct messaging, provided a behavioral anchor in a public climate of rumor and panic (Bandura, 1977; Drury, 2018). The recovery experience also underscored the limits of communication alone. Subsequent research has shown that restoring trust in institutions requires more than stabilization, it relies on accountability, reform, and continued transparency (Harvard Kennedy School, 2022).

Case Integration: Organizational Learning and Adaptive Economic Leadership

Both the Tylenol crisis and the 2008 financial sector meltdown underscore a fundamental truth: in organizational and economic crises, resilient outcomes hinge on swift, public modeling of integrity and adaptation. J&J's role modeling, including senior executives making themselves available for inquiry, modeling transparency, and prioritizing action over image, functioned as social proof that real change was underway (PBS, 2014; ScienceDirect, 2023). The direct engagement of stakeholders by senior executives, combined with robust corrective action, reset global expectations and set new, even higher standards for consumer protection (OU, 1997; Wikipedia, 2003).

The Fed and Treasury's management of the financial crisis was marked by strategic communication, public visibility, and the willingness to admit what was still unknown. Their credibility was built on regular updates, public Q&A sessions, and constant recalibration of actions based on rapidly changing feedback. Importantly, their leadership both reassured anxious markets and set a precedent for future crisis responses worldwide (Bernanke, 2015; HBS, 2023). At the organizational and institutional levels, visible acknowledgement of hardship, iterative correction, and inclusive dialogue have repeatedly proven essential for recovery, not only in financial contexts, but also in diverse sectors such as healthcare, technology, and manufacturing (Drury, 2018; Edmondson, 2019).

Leadership Toolbox: Organizational and Economic Crisis Resilience

Purpose: To guide leaders in establishing trust, credibility, and adaptive action in the face of organizational or economic disruption.

- **Transparency Mandate:** Communicate immediately, directly, and repeatedly to all stakeholders what is known, unknown, and being done.

- **Public Accountability:** Use regular briefings, public Q&As, and cross-sector representation to build sustained engagement and trust.

- **Visible Corrective Action:** Implement and demonstrate concrete steps (product recalls, process reforms, market interventions) while communicating the rationale.

- **Stakeholder-Inclusive Dialogue:** Establish mechanisms for gathering rapid feedback from employees, customers, or the public, integrate that input into continuous decision-making processes, and openly report results.

- **Solution-Focused Innovation:** Pair frank acknowledgement of risk with visible, iterative problem-solving (e.g., new safety features, rapid policy deployment).

- **Ethical Modeling:** Position senior leaders as primary spokespeople and actors, and ensure they model vulnerability, humility, and shared sacrifice.

- **Post-Event Reform:** After stabilization, systematically review actions, admit missteps, and implement structural changes for resilience and recovery long term.

13. MILITARY AND EXTREME ENVIRONMENTS

Shackleton's Antarctic Expedition: Psychological Leadership Under Prolonged Uncertainty

The 1914–1916 Imperial Trans-Antarctic Expedition undertaken by Ernest Shackleton endures as an iconic study of psychological leadership in the harshest possible conditions. When his ship, the Endurance, became trapped and then crushed by Antarctic ice, Shackleton was thrust into an impossible situation. He and his marooned crew faced the uncertainties of months stranded on drifting ice, survival uncertain, and hope in short supply (Drury, 2018; Shackleton.com, 2021). What followed was not only a tale of physical endurance but an unparalleled exercise in modeling resilience and morale for others.

Shackleton understood the fundamental principles of social learning well before they were formalized. He purposely modeled optimism, even when privately beset by despair, to signal hope and possibility to his crew (AQR International, 2024; Bandura, 1977). He established daily rituals to foster camaraderie and discipline. Rituals which included rotating leadership roles, sharing hardships, and fiercely protecting routine in the face of chaos (Climer Consulting, 2023). This strategic visibility meant that crew members, deprived of external information and comforts, mirrored his calm, stamina, and solution-focused approach rather than devolving into panic or hopelessness (Edmondson, 2019; Shackleton.com, 2021).

The defining example of psychological leadership came in April 1916, when Shackleton and five men set out across the storm-lashed Weddell Sea in a 22-foot open lifeboat, the *James Caird*, in an attempt to safely reach the whaling stations of South Georgia. The odds of safely traversing, and surviving, the almost 800-mile ribbon of shifting ice and freezing waters were abysmal. Yet Shackleton deliberately chose his companions not just for skill, but for temperament. He took those who were most restless or despairing, knowing that proximity to his steady presence would stabilize their morale. For 16 days, he kept a tone of measured confidence even as waves towered over their small craft and frostbite stiffened their hands. When they finally reached the island, he and two others trekked nonstop for 36 hours across uncharted, glaciated mountains to reach help. His first words upon arrival were not about his suffering, but his men still waiting. Within months, Shackleton returned for the rest of his crew, and not a single soul was lost.

His leadership toolbox included empathy and vulnerability, and these character traits daylighted through his knowing every crew member personally, and admitting uncertainty, yet refusing to let "despair become contagious" (Health Launchpad, 2025). He encouraged creative coping through debates, games, and shared meals to prevent mental and emotional collapse. Critically, Shackleton demonstrated flexible authority, sometimes imposing strict discipline, other times adapting to team needs, and always framing setbacks as shared and surmountable. The result was extraordinary. The *Endurance* saga remains one of the purest demonstrations of psychological safety and adaptive resilience under extreme conditions, an expedition that became a living laboratory of collective endurance and learned hope (Drury, 2018; Edmondson, 2019).

Modern Military Examples: U.S. Navy SEAL Crisis Training

Today's elite military units, including U.S. Navy SEALs, deliberately train and institutionalize psychological resilience for high-pressure, high-stakes environments. Their curriculum draws deeply from behavioral science, social learning theory, and the mental toughness model, recognizing that cognitive, emotional, and social habits determine survival as much as technical skill (Edmondson, 2019; Turvey, 2012).

From the onset, SEAL candidates are exposed to controlled adversity including prolonged cold, sleep deprivation, ambiguous orders, and simulated failure. Instructors model composure and adaptability, knowing that visible leader coping will be mirrored by trainees (Climer Consulting, 2023; Health Launchpad, 2025).

A key leadership practice is the concept of vulnerability in action. SEAL leaders debrief after failure, discussing emotional reactions and adaptive strategies as openly as tactical moves (AQR International, 2024). Leaders empower the most junior members to speak up about risks, thereby reinforcing psychological safety and promoting distributed leadership under pressure (Edmondson, 2019). Scenario-based training further encourages divergent thinking. Teams analyze failures, improvise in response to changing threats, and celebrate creative solutions, thereby cultivating an adaptive, feedback-rich culture.

One of the most striking operational examples came during *Operation Neptune Spear* in 2011, the mission to locate and eliminate Osama bin Laden.

The mission began with a catastrophic setback: one of the SEALs' Black Hawk helicopters crash-landed inside the compound. What could have spiraled into chaos instead became a masterclass in psychological steadiness. Team leaders immediately modeled composure and situational focus. No shouting, no panic, just clear, concise communication. Junior members took cues from that visible calm, maintaining discipline and adapting the plan in seconds. The SEALs successfully completed their objective, secured the target, and exfiltrated safely. Post-mission debriefs revealed that what preserved mission success was not superior weaponry or technology but practiced emotional regulation and mutual trust under duress.

Similarly, during humanitarian operations such as the 2009 *Captain Phillips hostage rescue*, SEAL Team Six demonstrated the duality of empathy and discipline that defines modern psychological leadership.

Negotiations were ongoing, tension razor-sharp, and any misstep could have cost lives. Yet the SEAL commander maintained visible steadiness, balancing empathy for the hostage's family with unflinching clarity in decision-making. The mission concluded with a perfect execution, three simultaneous sniper shots, each lethal, each precise. That outcome rested on collective calm, disciplined training, and a leader's ability to project confidence through chaos.

The SEAL ethos emphasizes both collective identity ("the team, the team, the team") and individual responsibility for resilience. Public and private rituals, including daily check-ins, peer recognition, and open acknowledgment of stress, serve to normalize recovery and fuel collective hope (Turvey, 2012). The social machinery of success is not ego or bravado, but rather humility, disciplined adaptability, and mutual modeling of psychological steadiness in the face of adversity.

Case Integration: Endurance, Adaptation, and Learned Resilience

Across eras, both polar exploration and special forces operations reveal the primacy of visible role modeling and proactive resilience-building in environments of catastrophic uncertainty. Shackleton's blend of authentic optimism, social bonding, and adaptive discipline enabled his men to maintain hope throughout 22 months of extreme ordeal, a beacon that has shaped leadership science ever since (AQR International, 2024; Shackleton.com, 2021). His routine, discipline, and emotional accessibility showed that hope is both taught and contagious.

Modern military leadership translates these principles into systematized practice. Navy SEALs and comparable units highlight the dangers of unchecked stoicism or cognitive rigidity, instead teaching future leaders to acknowledge fear and fatigue, support peer vulnerability, and pivot rapidly when confronted with failure (Drury, 2018; Turvey, 2012). Both domains confirm that resilience is not an innate trait, but an iterative, observable, and shareable group behavior set, requiring persistent modeling at every level.

By embedding these lessons, maintaining a focus on shared purpose, normalization of stress responses, and readiness to adapt, organizations can translate the rare heroism of Shackleton or elite soldiers into everyday resilience for teams facing long winters, complex competition, or relentless turbulence (Drury, 2018; Edmondson, 2019).

Leadership Toolbox: Resilient Leadership for Extreme Environments

Purpose: To guide leaders in fostering psychological stamina, visible coping, and adaptive modeling in settings of prolonged uncertainty and pressure.

- **Authentic Optimism Rituals:** Begin and end each day with explicit modeling of hope, and acknowledge difficulties, praise effort, and reframe setbacks as opportunities for learning.

- **Routine and Purpose:** Institute daily team rituals, from shared meals to formal "grit circles," that reinforce morale and unity.

- **Adaptive Authority Structure:** Rotate leadership where possible, empower dissent, and delegate problem-ownership to maintain group engagement.

- **Coping Strategy Visibility:** Freely narrate struggles, invite personal stories, and offer feedback on resilience, not just results.

- **Feedback and Peer Check-Ins:** Assign accountability partners to facilitate daily status sharing, mutual support, and the surfacing of hidden risks or signs of fatigue.

- **Creative Problem-Solving Sprints:** Schedule short, multidisciplinary brainstorms to build divergent thinking and stress-test solutions.

- **Normalize Debriefing:** Conduct honest, collective after-action reviews that center on both emotional adaptation and technical adjustment. Review, review, review!

- **Celebrate Mini-Wins:** Publicize, reward, and revisit small victories and adaptation moments that can serve as new models for group learning and growth.

PART III

Building the Edge of Calm
(Case Studies)

14. TRAINING THE CRISIS LEADER

Developing Emotional Regulation Skills

Mastering emotional regulation is fundamental to effective crisis leadership. Neuroscientific evidence confirms that stress responses activate the limbic system, narrowing cognition and triggering the fight-or-flight, freeze, or fawn survival pathways. This can impair executive functions such as decision-making, processing, and empathy (Drury, 2018; Edmondson, 2019). Therefore, crisis leaders must consistently cultivate emotional regulation as a core competency, not only to maintain their composure but to model resilience and security for their followers (Bavik et al., 2021; Goleman, 1995).

Breathing techniques offer a direct physiological lever to calm anxiety and restore focus. Leaders often start meetings or critical transitions with intentional controlled breathing exercises such as box breathing, the 4-7-8 method, or simple paced diaphragmatic breaths. These practices have been shown to reduce cortisol levels and activate the parasympathetic nervous system, effectively downshifting the stress response (Forbes, 2020; Tulane School of Social Work, 2024). Importantly, when leaders visibly engage in breathing exercises, they provide subconscious cues for their teams to regulate alongside them, fostering a culture of calm preparedness. (There are many examples of breathing exercises available on YouTube to study and practice.)

Cognitive reframing is equally essential. Leaders coach themselves, and sometimes their teams, to shift thought patterns from catastrophic "what if" scenarios to actionable "what can we do" frames, creating psychological space for creativity and problem-solving (Goleman, 1995). Reframing also involves openly acknowledging emotions while emphasizing agency and resilience and using affirmations such as "We have overcome challenges before" to reduce fear-based paralysis (Edmondson, 2019; Forbes, 2020).

Finally, **mindfulness** plays a crucial role. Mindfulness training, which includes meditation, body awareness, and deliberate attention control, enhances a leader's ability to observe their own stress cues and emotional impulses without judgement (Bavik et al., 2021). This self-awareness facilitates quicker, more reflective responses, which reduces emotional contagion and improves group dynamics (Drury, 2018). Mindfulness practices, when integrated into organizational routines (such as shift handoffs or daily briefings), empower entire teams to maintain mental clarity and collective psychological safety during prolonged crises.

Crisis Simulations and Scenario-Based Rehearsals

Emotional regulation skills are best honed within the pressure cooker of realistic crisis simulations. Extensive literature highlights the superiority of scenario-based training over purely theoretical learning towards the development of rapid decision-making, effective communication, and coordinated emotional regulation in uncertain situations (Center for Creative Leadership, 2025; Roberts et al., 2021). Simulations demand real-time adaptation to evolving, ambiguous conditions, strengthening not only individual competence but also, crucially, group cohesion and shared leadership capabilities.

Modern crisis simulations incorporate multifaceted elements such as time pressure, unexpected "injects," resource scarcity, conflicting information, and role ambiguity (Lacerenza et al., 2018). Teams engage in drills that sequence complex operational tasks alongside managing interpersonal conflict and emotional uncertainty, embodying the full spectrum of crisis challenge (Bavik et al., 2021). Rotating leadership roles during these exercises widens perspective, encourages empathy across operational silos, and reveals latent strengths or vulnerabilities (Edmondson, 2019).

Innovations in technology facilitate geographically dispersed, high-fidelity crisis training. Virtual reality and real-time scenario management platforms create immersive environments where leaders practice cognitive flexibility and emotional presence as dynamically as tactical decisions (Protecht Group, 2025; Weaver et al., 2010). Detailed after-action reviews, which utilize video feedback, tape recordings of communications, and biometric data, enhance self-awareness and team learning. Real time feedback is invaluable, allowing participants to pinpoint emotional spikes, successful regulation moments, and pathways to improved collective performance (Roberts et al., 2021).

The continuous cycle of rehearsal, feedback, and recalibration deeply embeds adaptive capacity and resilience into an organization's DNA. This is recognized in healthcare, military, aviation, and corporate sectors, where simulation training is no longer optional but foundational to crisis readiness (Edmondson, 2019; Tulane School of Social Work, 2024).

Crisis or simulation training does not need to be a highly advanced, technical, multifaceted undertaking. Simple crisis scenarios may be explored and practiced in tabletop settings and exercises, allowing participants to discuss decision-making, identify potential gaps, and reinforce communication and leadership skills without the pressure of a full-scale exercise.

Physical exercise scenarios may also be undertaken with the assistance of your local law enforcement or emergency response agencies, providing hands-on experience in real-world protocols, resource coordination, and crisis decision-making under controlled conditions.

The critical nature of crisis or simulation training is found in its ability to prepare individuals and teams to respond effectively under pressure, identify weaknesses before real events occur, and foster confidence, communication, and cohesion in high-stakes situations by gaming different scenarios in safe, controlled, and supportive environments.

The more you train, the less you need to depend on strained cognitive abilities during an actual crisis. Both physical exercises and tabletop scenarios help ingrain instinctive reactions, muscle memory, and decision-making habits, so that when a real emergency arises, your responses are automatic and reliable.

The Role of Cross Training and "Post-Mortem"

Cross-training expands crisis readiness by nurturing versatile, cognitively flexible leaders who understand and appreciate multiple operational perspectives, pressures, and emotional landscapes (Faraj & Xiao, 2006; Laurillard, 2008). Rotating leaders through different crisis roles, whether technical, communicative, or logistical, builds empathy and anticipatory skill. Such exposure helps prevent silos and improves mutual trust, especially important because real crises rarely – if ever – respect organizational boundaries (Protecht Group, 2025).

Cross-trained teams demonstrate agility. When gaps or overloads emerge in one sector during a crisis, others can rapidly fill the void. Experience in diverse roles also enhances divergent thinking and complex problem-solving by enriching mental frameworks (Brandfolder, 2023; Doodle, 2025). Organizations known for excellence in crisis response intentionally schedule annual role rotations or "shadowing," reinforcing that leadership is a shared, dynamic process.

Completing the training cycle, post-mortem reviews, or after-action reviews are crucial. These are safe, blame-free, structured group discussions conducted promptly, with all in attendance after exercises or incidents to reflect on both technical successes and failures, as well as emotional responses and team dynamics (Edmondson, 2019; Lacerenza et al., 2018). Questions routinely explore when emotional regulation faltered or flourished and how leadership presence influenced group cohesion and adaptability (Roberts et al., 2021). Post-mortems transform raw experience into explicit, actionable "lessons learned," driving continuous development of crisis competence.

Post-mortem reviews are not limited only to the evaluation and betterment of crisis response. For example, imagine a team tasked with launching a new customer-facing mobile app. After the launch, a post-mortem review would gather developers, designers, product managers, and support staff to evaluate the project from start to finish. The team might identify that the beta testing phase successfully caught critical bugs, a process worth repeating in future projects. Conversely, they could note that communication between design and development was inconsistent, leading to last-minute changes that delayed the release. By documenting these lessons – what worked, what didn't, and why – the team can implement concrete improvements, such as standardized design handoff protocols or more frequent cross-team check-ins, ensuring the next app launch is smoother, faster, and more effective.

High-reliability organizations embed cross-training and post-mortem practices into strategic talent pipelines and ongoing team culture (Center for Creative Leadership, 2025). This holistic approach transforms not only crisis readiness, but many other aspects of business operations from episodic drills – or routine – into a living, adaptive capability, where efficiency and emotional regulation are both taught and reinforced in real-time.

Case Integration: Building Capacity Through Integrated Training

Healthcare, military, and emergency management organizations provide compelling evidence for the power of integrated emotional and scenario training. Trauma centers conduct complex drills rotating physicians, nurses, and logisticians through different roles, often pairing intensive technical practice with emotional regulation coaching and resilience discussion (Roberts et al., 2021). Navy SEAL teams integrate leadership rotation with both physical and emotional stress inoculation, complemented by immediate debriefs on coping and adjustment strategies (Turvey, 2012).

Organizations that pioneer crisis management recognize that when emotional competence and operational rehearsal advance in tandem, and when learning from every success and failure is normalized, teams develop not only technical readiness but also the psychological grounding essential to thrive under pressure (Bavik et al., 2021; Edmondson, 2019).

Case Example 1: **Johnson & Johnson's Tylenol Recall (1982)**

When seven people in Chicago died after taking cyanide-laced Tylenol capsules, Johnson & Johnson faced a potentially company-ending crisis. CEO James Burke's emotionally regulated leadership became a benchmark in corporate crisis response. Rather than reacting defensively, Burke centered communication around empathy, transparency, and public safety, anchored by the company's Credo, which prioritized customer welfare above profits. He maintained his composure in front of the press, using calm and factual framing ("We will not rest until we know what happened"), and directed a full nationwide recall, which cost over $100 million.

Post-crisis debriefs (aftercare) emphasized the importance of emotional transparency and value-driven decision-making as essential components of effective crisis leadership. The company's swift, composed, and ethical response not only restored public trust but transformed corporate crisis management globally, embedding emotional regulation, moral clarity, and stakeholder communication as inseparable aspects of executive training (Berg & Rob, 1992; Fink, 1983; Greyser, 1982).

Case Example 2: **New Zealand's Christchurch Hospital Earthquake Response (2011)**

During the 6.3 magnitude earthquake that struck Christchurch, hospital teams exemplified the power of emotional regulation under extreme pressure. With power outages, collapsed infrastructure, and an influx of mass casualties, leaders implemented immediate breathing and mindfulness protocols among trauma teams to maintain calm amid chaos. Surgeons rotated leadership roles, allowing exhausted colleagues to rest and reorient. After-action debriefs conducted within 24 hours focused not just on procedural breakdowns but on emotional load-sharing, leading to the institutionalization of mindfulness and resilience training in New Zealand's healthcare crisis curriculum (Canterbury District Health Board, 2012; O'Toole, 2017).

Case Example 3: **Apollo 13 Mission Control Crisis (1970)**

When an oxygen tank exploded aboard Apollo 13, NASA's Mission Control faced an unprecedented life-or-death emergency in real time. Flight Director Gene Kranz demonstrated masterful emotional regulation, refusing panic and reframing the situation with the now-famous phrase: *"Let's work the problem, people. Let's not make things worse by guessing."* His calm tone and cognitive reframing set the emotional climate for the entire team. Through collective composure and structured debriefs after the mission, NASA embedded emotional regulation and communication discipline into its simulation and leadership training for future missions (Kranz, 1999; Tiwari, 2015).

Leadership Toolbox: Embedding Emotional and Scenario Mastery

Purpose: To provide crisis leaders and organizations with strategies for developing, reinforcing, and sustaining emotional regulation and adaptive scenario leadership.

- **Routine Emotional Check-Ins:** Dedicate a few minutes at shift changes, meetings, or briefings to explore current stress levels and discuss effective regulation strategies.

  A simple and effective stress regulation strategy a boss might pass on is the *box breathing technique.* The boss could explain it like this: *"When you feel overwhelmed, try this simple exercise: inhale slowly for a count of four, hold your breath for four, exhale for four, and then hold again for four. Repeat for several cycles – at least five or ten times. It helps calm the nervous system, sharpen focus, and reset your stress response so you can approach challenges more clearly."*

Although many examples like this exist, this technique is quick, evidence-based, and can be done at a desk or even before a high-pressure meeting, making it practical for employees in any role.

- **High-Fidelity Scenario Calendar:** Implement scheduled, multidimensional crisis simulations that escalate in complexity and span diverse operational and emotional roles.

- **Role Rotation Programs:** Establish formal cycles that enable leaders and staff to train regularly in roles outside their primary areas of expertise, thereby enhancing empathy and agility.

- **Structured After-Action Reviews (AARs):** After real or simulated events or training, conduct inclusive, blame-free sessions focusing on both tactical and emotional lessons.

- **Peer Feedback Networks:** Organize feedback pairs or groups that focus on emotional regulation behaviors and scenario performance – the buddy system.

- **Learning Journals:** Encourage leaders and teams to document emotional triggers, coping successes, evolving scenarios, and review outcomes to foster growth and development.

- **Visible Modeling:** Leaders should openly share coping methods, learning curves, and adaptive strategies, setting norms of vulnerability and resilience. What worked, what didn't, and why.

- **Adaptive Scenario Updates:** Continuously refine training scenarios based on post-mortem insights, emerging risks, and new scientific understanding.

15. CRAFTING COMMUNICATION UNDER STRESS

Building "Command Presence" Without Authoritarianism

The crucible of a crisis exposes not just the content of a leader's message, but the embodied power of presence itself. The notion of "command presence" conjures images of a rigid posture, a stern vocal tone, or an imposing, room-filling authority. Yet, in effective crisis leadership, true command presence is something altogether different (Bavik et al., 2021; Goleman, 1995). It is not an autocrat's bark nor the slow drum of panic; rather, it is the cultivated ability to project confidence, clarity, and safety, anchoring the crowd even in the worst storm (Drury, 2018; Edmondson, 2019).

Command presence rests in the quiet certainties. The leader who enters a room and signals with a deliberate, unhurried gait that "I will not be rushed by chaos." The cadence of speech, a steady, measured delivery with intentional silences, has the same physiological effect on a crowd as a collective deep breath. Audiences, consciously or not, synchronize to the rhythm of the leader's emotional climate, echoing what social neuroscientists refer to as emotional entrainment (Bavik et al., 2021; Goleman, 1995).

Importantly, command presence under stress is not about dominance. It is about authenticity and empathy without bluster. The gentle assertion of control with respect for the autonomy and intelligence of others. Leaders who bark, threaten, or grandstand breed resentment and

119

resistance, not trust (Edmondson, 2019). True command presence instead starts from within. A visible self-control and composure that becomes the "psychological ground" upon which anxious followers can step (Forbes, 2020).

The most successful leaders adapt their presence to suit the context. Sometimes command presence is soft-spoken, even at a whisper level, as with Jacinda Ardern's televised addresses during the New Zealand COVID-19 crisis, where empathy and restrained strength outperformed any show of bravado (Doodle, 2025). Other times, it is kinetic. Giuliani walking amidst the dust of Ground Zero, taking questions and giving direction, never over-claiming certainty but not retreating from the crowd's gaze (Drury, 2018; NYT, 2007).

Crafting Short, Direct Messages for Memory Retention

In the midst of a crisis, the human brain struggles to process complexity or jargon. Research from cognitive science and emergency communication indicates that under stress, working memory capacity decreases. Recall is limited to the most basic, simplest, and most frequently repeated instructions (Bavik et al., 2021; Weick & Sutcliffe, 2015). Thus, the art of communication under stress is the art of radical concision.

Experts recommend that core messages be delivered in brief, concrete phrases, ideally no more than one or two actionable ideas at a time (Flin, 1996; Goleman, 1995). This is known as "beachhead communication." Give people the minimum, sharpest information they need to take the next step, and repeat it consistently. After-action reviews of disasters, from the Boston Marathon bombings to the Fukushima evacuation, reveal that survivors who recall clear, direct messages fare better in navigating confusion and uncertainty (Edmondson, 2019; Roberts et al., 2021).

Repetition is key. Studies of crisis memory indicate that it may take three or more exposures to a message before it is encoded and retrievable in real-time (Bavik et al., 2021; Weick & Sutcliffe, 2015). The language must be as concrete and sensory as possible: "Exit to the left. Stay low.

Move now." Ambiguity kills, as does technical complexity. Use plain words every time ("danger," "safe," "wait," "go").

Crafting for memory also means structuring messages with redundancy. Use both spoken word and simple visuals such as, a bold color-coded sign, a hand signal, a repeated gesture. If sending alerts or digital comms, keep messages no longer than a tweet, and do not embed multiple action steps in one instruction (Protecht Group, 2025).

A well-crafted crisis message is a linguistic lifeline – short enough to survive panic, precise enough to cut through noise, and memorable enough to be shared by word of mouth when technology or communication lines fail (Weick & Sutcliffe, 2015).

Practical Speaking Techniques

Moving from theory to practice, leaders under pressure benefit from a specific toolkit of speaking behaviors and techniques, designed to maximize understanding and psychological impact.

1. Breathing and Centering: Before speaking, take at least two visible breath cycles, using slow diaphragmatic breathing, to lower cortisol, steady the voice, and subconsciously anchor the audience (Goleman, 1995; Tulane, 2024). This centers attention, projects self-control, and sets the tone before a word is spoken.

2. Use of Name and Eye Contact: If addressing a small or mid-sized group, start by saying names or roles aloud as a bridge. "Team A, this is your directive," and make authentic eye contact. Shifting eye contact among a crowd spreads emotional regulation and prevents the "lecture trance" that can quickly shut down active listening (Bavik et al., 2021; Edmondson, 2019).

3. Intentional Pauses: After giving an instruction or statement, pause for three slow counts. This allows listener's brains to catch up and signals the importance of your words. Strategic silence also provides others with the psychological space to process, reflect, and request clarification (Forbes, 2020; Weaver et al., 2010).

4. Physical Anchoring: Use posture to reinforce authority without threat. Stand upright but relaxed, feet planted for stability, with open hands when possible. Avoid closed, defensive, or aggressive postures. Research has found that micro-expressions and a "soft gaze" (relaxed yet attentive eyes) can lower defensive postures in a group (Doodle, 2025; Goleman, 1995).

5. Vocal Modulation: Tone, pace, and volume should be modulated based on the audience and event urgency. Speak from the diaphragm for resonance. Lower the tone slightly as urgency increases, but avoid rapid-fire delivery, which can heighten anxiety (Bavik et al., 2021; Tulane, 2024). Use rhythmic, repetitive phrasing to create a psychological anchor: "We move together, we stay together, we act together."

6. Message Repetition and Redundancy: Repeat key instructions verbatim, ideally three times, at distinct points in your communication. Reinforce with gestures, written words, or environmental cues (Protecht Group, 2025; Weick & Sutcliffe, 2015).

7. Explicit Permission and Queries: Invite clarifying questions or repeat-back, "Who can tell me what we're doing next?" This technique surfaces confusion before it causes danger and enlists group members as extensions of the communication chain (Roberts et al., 2021).

8. Authentic Affect and Empathy: Name emotion out loud, "I see this is frightening," or "I know you are exhausted," then pair it with targeted direction. Emotional acknowledgement increases compliance, trust, and memory retention (Drury, 2018; Goleman, 1995).

9. Avoiding Jargon: Strip language of acronyms, technical terms, and filler words. Choose "This is what you must do now" over "I recommend consideration of the following protocol" (Edmondson, 2019; Flin, 1996).

10. Narrative and Imagery: Where helpful, use short stories or sharp mental images. "When you hear the alarm, picture your safe exit as the blue door on the left." Brief, vivid cues aid recall under adrenaline.

Leaders must rehearse these techniques under simulated stress. Crisis simulation training, which combines physical exertion, auditory chaos, and organizational pressure, reveals weaknesses in speaking or listening habits that would otherwise go unnoticed. Teams that train together in calm develop a shared code and cadence for using these tools when the stakes are real.

Case Integration: From Command Presence to Lasting Memory

Consider the real-world case of field hospitals activated during the initial COVID-19 surge. Overwhelmed staff operated in a mask-concealed state of chaos, with changing guidelines and high emotional volatility. Supervisors who meticulously modeled command presence, a steady voice, visible breath, and repeated eye contact were rated by teams as the most trustworthy and had the fewest communication breakdowns during shifts (Edmondson, 2019; Roberts et al., 2021). Nurses who repeated patient care instructions three times reported fewer errors and a greater sense of predictability and calm.

In mass evacuations from wildfires or hurricanes, research finds that the groups receiving crisp, short messages ("Go north. Use the green signs. Wait for instructions.") evacuated faster and more safely than those who heard ambiguous or multi-part guidance (Flin, 1996; Weick & Sutcliffe, 2015). After-action data from the Boston Marathon bombings highlights that simple, redundant commands effectively reduced panic and chaos, enabling even untrained crowd members to become reliable communicators and pass clear instructions to others as technology failed (Roberts et al., 2021).

These examples collectively illustrate that the impact of crisis leadership extends far beyond immediate operational outcomes.

Command presence, emotional regulation, and clear, repetitive communication do not merely prevent mistakes, they shape the psychological environment, creating predictability, trust, and cohesion under pressure. Whether in hospitals, during wildfire evacuations, or at mass gatherings under threat, leaders who combine calm, authentic, empathetic authority with structured guidance can convert chaos into coordinated action. The lasting memory of such leadership, encoded in both team performance and individual perception, becomes a blueprint for future crisis response. It embeds resilience, adaptability, and confidence into the very culture of the organization (Edmondson, 2019; Roberts et al., 2021; Weick & Sutcliffe, 2015).

Leadership Toolbox: Speaking Presence Under Pressure

Purpose: To give leaders and teams a step-by-step practice for communicating with clarity, calm, and retention value in high-stress conditions.

- **Pre-Briefing Rituals:** Gather teams for two minutes of silent breathing and intentional silence before every high-stakes announcement or brief.

- **Message Mapping:** Boil each communication down to a single, specific call to action, structuring statements so that the most essential words come first.

- **Visual and Gestural Pairing:** Use color-coded cards, hand signals, or other physical cues in conjunction with spoken commands to reinforce memory.

- **Repetition Protocol:** Script and stick to the "three times, three ways" rule for critical information: spoken, written, and signaled.

- **Active Clarification:** Formalize "repeat-back" or "teach-back" routines at the end of every brief and randomly ask team members to restate or show next steps.

- **Feedback Calibration:** Conduct a debrief after every communication event, incorporating peer review and self-coaching, with a focus on body language, clarity, and emotional presence. What was confusing or unclear?

- **Scenario Rehearsal:** Rotate roles during simulation exercises so everyone has practice giving and receiving urgent instructions in rapidly changing, real-world conditions.

- **Normalize Emotion:** Routinely call out the pressure, name the fear, then pair with clear direction: "This is hard. Here's our move."

- **Train for Silence:** Practice pausing after key instructions and watching for comprehension before moving on. Silence embeds learning.

- **Micro-Storytelling:** Include ultra-short, repeatable stories or vivid mental images to create hooks for memory under stress when appropriate.

16. TRUST, EMPATHY, AND PSYCHOLOGICAL SAFETY

The Quiet Heartbeat of Group Survival

When the world shakes, it is the small acts that hold people together. A word, a look, a light touch on the shoulder, a single, genuine gesture of empathy can tilt an entire room away from panic and toward resolve (Drury, 2018; Edmondson, 2019; Goleman, 1995). Trust, fragile as spun glass, can be painstakingly built over time and then shattered in a moment of neglect or falsehood (Center for Creative Leadership, 2025; Edmondson, 2019). Psychological safety is not built on charisma or competence alone, it is the accumulation of thousands of tiny signals that say, "You can be fully human here. You will not be left behind."

Groups facing stress are like organisms under threat. Their survival hinges on cohesion. The leaders who foster genuine trust and belonging do so not by decree but by a deep, visible empathy. From military outposts to makeshift medical wards, from C-suites during market collapse to field shelters battered by storms, the best leaders are those who understand how profoundly small, timely acts of empathy and ritual can impact the collective mind (Bavik et al., 2021; Edmondson, 2019).

Small Acts of Empathy in High Tension

Empathy is most vital not when times are good, but when fear and doubt radiate through a group. Research shows that leaders who notice individual anxiety, who look up, connect eyes, and pause to ask "How are you?" in the midst of chaos, trigger a cascade of biological and psychological benefits that ripple outward (Bavik et al., 2021; Goleman, 1995). A hand's squeeze at a triage tent, a nurse's voice-over at a masked bedside, the briefest moment of shared laughter, such acts ground people, interrupting the cycle of anxiety and signaling, "I see you."

These gestures matter more than any formal address. Studies in disaster psychology and military leadership alike reveal that when leaders take a second to acknowledge fear, simply by naming it, a sense of safety grows almost instantly within the group (Drury, 2018; Edmondson, 2019). Jacinda Ardern captured this in her consistent, comforting broadcasts during the pandemic, repeating, "This is hard. We will get through it together." Such words don't solve every problem, but they allow emotion to surface and keep loneliness at bay (Doodle, 2025).

Empathy, practiced in micro-moments, becomes the invisible glue of group decision-making and innovation under crisis. Teams led by authentic, warm leaders report fewer errors, lower burnout, and a greater willingness to surface disagreement or problems. These traits are the key predictors of resilience and should serve as a thermometer of group performance and cohesion (Bavik et al., 2021; Edmondson, 2019). When empathy is consistently modeled, it signals that every voice matters, encourages constructive conflict, and transforms stress into adaptive problem-solving rather than paralysis. In essence, empathy doesn't just soften interactions, it strengthens the team's capacity to respond, recover, and thrive amid uncertainty.

How Trust Can Be Built or Destroyed in Seconds

High-stress moments are accelerants for trust; they can either catalyze lifelong bonds or crack years of careful work wide open. Trust is established when leaders combine presence with transparency, acknowledge uncertainty, and accept responsibility for both their decisions and their communication (Center for Creative Leadership, 2025; Edmondson, 2019). A single honest admission, "I don't know, but we're working on it," can deepen credibility far faster than polished assurances that ring false (Goleman, 1995).

Yet trust can also be lost in the blink of an eye. When a leader betrays a team's vulnerability or fails to follow through on a promise, the sense of belonging is instantly replaced by distress signals. Withdrawal, obstacles to learning, and diminished voice become prevalent. Disasters such as Hurricane Katrina and the COVID-19 pandemic have demonstrated how executive hedging, visible double standards, or the concealment of vital information can fuel suspicion and disengagement among the populous (Drury, 2018; Edmondson, 2019).

In the digital age, where rumors spread quickly and credibility is always one message away from collapse, consistency and personal modeling are everything. Repeated research confirms that groups remember not speeches, but unguarded moments, those who stayed with them late, who admitted error when it was hard, and who made space for questions when it was important to the individuals (Center for Creative Leadership, 2025; Doodle, 2025).

Rituals and Symbols That Reinforce Belonging in Groups Under Stress

Belonging is not a side effect of competence, it is the result of deliberately designed rituals, spaces, and symbols that reconnect a group to its identity and shared meaning. Neuroscience and behavioral studies show that people in danger instinctively turn toward rituals which might include physical routines, words, songs, totems, and anything that may reaffirm a sense of "us" and buffer against the terror of isolation (Drury, 2018; Edmondson, 2019).

Consider the small routines in crisis wards. Posting daily gratitude boards, team huddles with mutual encouragement, the passing of a token, or a written affirmation at shift change. In firefighting, the shared donning of gear, the ritual check-in, and even the habitual knock on a fire truck before departure signal shared purpose and calm, subconsciously binding the group together (Weaver et al., 2010). In military history, colors and mottos have long symbolized belonging, and even in digital workforces, simple practices persist. Group signoffs, "camera-on" rituals, or digital high-fives can quickly ground a scattered team (Roberts et al., 2021).

Symbols are powerfully sticky. During the Ebola response, colored wristbands marked team membership, uniting new and veteran workers. At the Boston Marathon, finishers' medals became collective markers of resilience (Edmondson, 2019). Belonging also thrives in language. Leaders who use "we," who tell origin stories, incorporate humor, or share inside jokes, build lasting bridges for their team through the uncertainty of the event (Drury, 2018).

This practice is especially prevalent when a threat persists over weeks or months. Organizations that systematize rituals and symbols, small, inclusive, and authentic, report greater psychological safety, lower attrition, and clearer collective goals (Bavik et al., 2021; Edmondson, 2019).

Case Integration: Empathy, Trust, and Ritual in Action

Crises large and small showcase how human connection under stress shapes outcomes. At the initial onset of the COVID-19 pandemic, hospitals that trained supervisors to explicitly check for stress, invite stories, and validate fear reported measurable drops in staff anxiety and burnout (Bavik et al., 2021; Edmondson, 2019). At emergency management agencies and city fire departments, "hope boards," mutual aid shifts, and peer shout-outs ensured that even in exhaustion, people saw their work and emotions reflected back to them.

However, lapses in empathy or trust can also significantly shape outcomes. Hurricane Katrina's aftermath is a textbook case of trust destruction. Leaders who failed to acknowledge uncertainty, ignored vulnerable voices, and concealed logistical breakdowns left communities fractured for years (Drury, 2018). By contrast, the rapid integration of group rituals and honest, "us over I" communication in Japanese communities following the Fukushima disaster helped rebuild ties quickly, and enabled collective adaptation (Edmondson, 2019; Roberts et al., 2021).

Military units on deployment, combating the isolation and cumulative stress of long-term threat, rely on nightly rituals of shared meals, mutual checkups, and symbolic tokens passed down over generations, all acts proven to buffer against trauma and accelerate and reinforce group cohesion (Weaver et al., 2010). Corporate case studies demonstrate that even in virtual teams under pressure, visible displays of empathy, public shout-outs, daily gratitude postings, paired mentorship, and sharing group origin stories predict lower error rates and a greater willingness to seek help (Center for Creative Leadership, 2025; Doodle, 2025).

Leadership Toolbox: Applying Empathy, Trust, and Ritual in Crisis

Purpose: To guide leaders and teams in systematically embedding trust, empathy, and belonging into daily crisis practice.

- **Micro-Empathy Rituals:** Begin and end meetings with a personal "weather check." Encourage sharing a word or gesture to name how the group is feeling.

- **Transparency Anchors:** Normalize quick, candid check-ins where leaders openly acknowledge uncertainty, forecast next steps, and invite any questions without fear of reprisal.

- **Visible Consistency:** Make promises you only intend to keep. When mistakes occur, admit them immediately and model humility by thanking others for pointing out blind spots.

- **Daily Ritualization:** Institute recurring, small group rituals, gratitude rounds, team signoffs, check-in circles, and rotating "shout-out" moments across roles.

- **Symbolic Belonging:** Establish and distribute shared items, such as wristbands, pins, digital badges, challenge coins, or mantra cards, that signal group identity and continuity.

- **Story and Language Building:** Regularly tell and retell the origin story, highlight acts of mutual care, and use inclusive language to foster "we-ness."

- **Emotionally-Safe Post-Mortems:** After each incident or milestone, create space to discuss emotions, praise adaptations, and surface what trust-building acts made a difference.

- **Continuous Feedback Loops:** Solicit peer input on trust and belonging. Integrate insights into strategic planning and culture-building sessions to inform and enhance decision-making.

- **Peer Support Pairing:** Match team members in rotating dyads for daily or weekly check-ins focused on support and encouragement.

17. ADAPTABILITY AND CONTINUOUS LEARNING

Why Adaptability Is the Lifeline

When the ground shifts beneath organizations, when plans implode mid-flight, facts mutate by the hour, and pressure squeezes error from the cracks, what determines survival isn't lineage, tradition, or even technical prowess, but the muscle memory of adaptability (Edmondson, 2019; Weaver, 2010; Weick & Sutcliffe, 2015). Unlike brittle systems wedded to yesterday's map, adaptable teams and leaders treat crisis as a proving ground for creative evolution. They don't just bounce back; they bounce forward, forging new strategies and cultures from the ashes of setbacks (Drury, 2018; Edmondson, 2019).

At the core of this learning is a living culture of inquiry and constructive dissent. A visceral rejection of stagnation, groupthink, and blame. Adaptability is not soft accommodation. It is the discipline of turning after-action reviews into a resilience loop, normalizing dissent as fuel for option generation, and reframing adversity as the seedbed for innovation (Bavik et al., 2021; Center for Creative Leadership, 2025; Protech Group, 2021).

After-Action Reviews and Resilience Loops

The strongest teams and organizations make review not an afterthought, but a ritual, a living circuit that powers ongoing learning. The after-action review (AAR) originated from high-stakes settings, including elite military units, air traffic control, and emergency medicine. In these situations, the margin for error is razor-thin, the stakes are life and death, and wisdom is weaponized only if it can be rapidly cycled back into new behavior (Edmondson, 2019; Lacerenza et al., 2018).

A successful AAR does far more than catalog mistakes. It maps what happened, why, what worked, what failed, and, most critically, how the team can adapt next time (Weick & Sutcliffe, 2015). Everyone speaks, regardless of rank or ego. The best AARs begin with a leader's invitation to honesty, "Where did I mess up? What did I miss?" They are blame-free zones in which candor is rewarded over comfort, and emotional responses are as valid data points as technical outcomes (Edmondson, 2019).

But resilience is not born of review alone. The loop closes only if findings and insights from AARs are acted upon, including the development of new playbooks, drills, updates to checklists and decision trees, and even cultural or workflow shifts (Bavik et al., 2021). Mature organizations track, even visually, their learning and adjustments. A whiteboard in the break room outlining lessons from the last simulation, a digital log or spreadsheet in the safety binder for tracking real-time feedback that all have access to from partners during a crisis, and formal process improvements publicized in quarterly reviews.

Meaningful AARs always return to a basic prompt: What did we do? What did we learn? And what will we do differently going forward? The loop is only closed when an explicit feedback path takes new lessons from one event into practice and then back into review. This recursive process inoculates teams against the corrosive effects of failure (Edmondson, 2019; Lacerenza et al., 2018).

Encouraging Divergent Perspectives in Planning

In high-stakes environments, consensus can be deadly. Groupthink, the overvaluing of harmony at the expense of challenge, blinds teams to risk, narrows the solution landscape, and renders plans brittle (Drury, 2018; Edmondson, 2019). The antidote is structured divergence. Plan environments where dissent is not only tolerated but demanded, where multiple perspectives are surfaced and explored before decisions are finalized (Weick & Sutcliffe, 2015).

This doesn't mean endless debate for its own sake. The most adaptive teams empower members to formally challenge assumptions, voice alternative analyses, and propose "outlier" options, often via "red teams," rotating devil's advocates, and explicit scenario testing (Center for Creative Leadership, 2025; Roberts et al., 2021). These mechanisms foster cognitive diversity and create a safe space for people to challenge the dominant logic without incurring emotional penalties (Bavik et al., 2021).

Explicit protocols are required. Begin planning meetings with an expectation that every critical decision will be tested by structured dissent. Encourage cross-departmental involvement in scenario construction. Create formal round-robins for unorthodox suggestions. Senior leaders must model openness and create opportunities whereby they are repeatedly thanking team members for raising uncomfortable possibilities, even if those options aren't ultimately chosen (Edmondson, 2019).

Studies show that organizations with built-in divergent thinking not only anticipate threats and adapt more quickly in volatile conditions, but they also enjoy higher morale, stronger engagement, and a greater sense of psychological safety (Bavik et al., 2021; Drury, 2018).

Reframing Crises as Opportunities for Innovation

Perhaps the greatest lever for continuous learning is reframing crises as an opportunity. Not in the saccharine, empty platitude sense, but as a lived commitment to extracting solutions, process improvements, and creative leaps from adversity (Center for Creative Leadership, 2025; Goleman, 1995). Adaptive leaders narrate crises not just as an obstacle course but as a laboratory, as a source of data, a training ground for new techniques, and a crucible for organizational growth (Center for Creative Leadership, 2025; Goleman, 1995; Weaver, 2010).

Reframing begins with executive language. Leaders who ask, "What does this teach us?" and "How do we build forward from here?" invite the group to stay curious, surfacing underlying causes and new possibilities more quickly than leaders who default to blame or loss-avoidance (Edmondson, 2019; Forbes, 2020). Strength and creativity routines like "solution sprints," after-crisis hackathons, action learning sets, and the public celebration of "fast failures" as learning moments help to institutionalize and affirm a culture of innovation.

Innovation is not just technological; it is often social and procedural, suggesting new rituals for check-ins, fresh communication protocols, or the repurposing of legacy tools in novel ways. The Boston Marathon bombings catalyzed advances in crowd safety protocols and digital emergency messaging. The SARS and COVID-19 outbreaks forced healthcare systems globally to redesign triage pathways, telemedicine portals, and implement cross-functional collaboration almost overnight (Edmondson, 2019; Weick & Sutcliffe, 2015).

By deliberately crafting moments in which teams are rewarded for inventiveness and recognized for surfacing creative alternatives, organizations embed adaptability into the fabric of their culture (Bavik et al., 2021; Center for Creative Leadership, 2025; Protech Group, 2021). Don't reward your team just for "getting it right the first time," as empty platitudes do nothing toward the development of team strength and unity. Crises thus become accelerators of transformation, not just threats to survive.

Deep Dive: From After-Action to Innovation "Flywheels"

The deepest learning cultures borrow from elite military and aviation routines, turning after-action loops into innovation flywheels – a self-reinforcing cycle of continuous improvement. In elite fire departments and trauma centers, for example, every shift and incident ends with a shared recap in which line-level staff and senior leadership share equal footing. These moments are opportunities to uncover hidden near-misses, elevate clever improvisations from the field, and make real-time updates to playbooks and safety binders before the next emergency strikes (Edmondson, 2019; Roberts et al., 2021).

Organizations like NASA and high-reliability health systems document and distribute "micro learnings" across sites, cross-pollinating ideas from one team or locale to every sister unit. This breaks down silos while rapidly flattening learning curves. The protocol isn't only to learn from error, but to codify newfound best practices, transforming every small fix into shared institutional muscle (Lacerenza et al., 2018).

Crucially, these flywheels also articulate the emotionally intelligent side of learning: they reward those who admit uncertainty, celebrate the naming of blind spots, and normalize both vulnerability and recovery as core professional strengths (Edmondson, 2019).

Building Adaptive Story and Narrative

Story is the backbone of learning and reinvention. Adaptive organizations use narrative to reframe stumbles as steppingstones. Leaders re-tell the tale of a failed launch that seeded a new business line or a miscommunication that unraveled an old process in favor of greater clarity (Goleman, 1995). Just as rituals and symbols matter for belonging, stories of "lessons well-earned" become the cognitive glue that embeds adaptability into the group psyche.

These stories must be real, honest, unpolished, and participatory. Invite team members to narrate how a crisis changed their work for the better. Regular "retrospective rounds," open-mic learning sessions, or digital journals capture insights from every seat, not just the C-suite. The innovation culture grows more robust when everyone can point to stories where change, rather than conformity, prevail (Center for Creative Leadership, 2025).

Organizational storytelling is richest when it cuts across hierarchy and function. When every role, from support staff to executive, can voice what they have noticed and what they hope to try next. Over time, these stories become the unofficial curriculum of the learning organization (Drury, 2018; Edmondson, 2019).

Case Integration: Adaptability in Action

During the 2010 Icelandic volcano eruption, European air carriers and regulators confronted a challenge never seen before. Mass airspace closures, complex contingency planning, and a blizzard of conflicting data. After-action reviews revealed both blind spots and creative improvisations (Edmondson, 2019). Within days, collaborative platforms had been established across airlines, between meteorologists, and governments freely exchanged data without the usual bureaucratic wrangling, fundamentally changing the available playbooks worldwide for responding to future natural disasters.

Hospitals swamped by COVID-19 rapidly repurposed strategies from other sectors. Simulation hospitals became classrooms for remote learning. Logistics teams borrowed principles from just-in-time manufacturing to manage PPE, ward teams rotated roles under new "buddy systems" to ensure cross-trained backup amid fatigue (Bavik et al., 2021; Center for Creative Leadership, 2025). These rapid adaptations exemplify how crisis-driven innovation can dissolve traditional boundaries, tear down imaginary walls, and accelerate organizational learning.

In the wake of major hurricanes, cities with established after-action cultures managed debris and restoration more efficiently, having already codified lessons about adaptive sourcing of supplies and neighbor-to-neighbor relief. Crowdsourced updates from residents informed citywide playbooks in real time, illustrating the exponential power of distributed, inclusive learning systems (Drury, 2018).

Leadership Toolbox: Embedding Adaptability and Continuous Learning

Purpose: To institutionalize feedback, diversity of thought, and the reframing of crisis as a platform for perpetual innovation.

- **After-Action Review Protocols:** Structure every incident, drill, and project wrap-up with regular, all-voices reviews. Track not only what happened, but why, and how procedures or plans will be improved.

- **Resilience Logbooks:** Institutionalize digital or physical "lesson learned" journals, updated after every challenge (add them to your safety binder). Make them accessible to all staff and review them quarterly as a team with the objective of turning the best ideas into operational updates.

- **Divergence Boards:** Create visible, rotating spaces (physical or virtual) for surfacing dissenting views, wild ideas, and non-consensus options in real time.

- **Red Teaming and Devil's Advocacy:** Assign roles or small teams to intentionally challenge mainstream assumptions in planning, drills, and reviews.

- **Solution Sprints:** After setbacks or surprises, run fast "design hackathons" or brainstorming rounds explicitly aimed at generating actionable innovations from crisis data.

- **Narrative Integration:** Build story-sharing into meetings, post-mortems, and digital platforms, and regularly feature team member's stories of adaptation, stress, and discovery.

- **Formalize Change Cycles:** Ensure every major or significant lesson learned is not only absorbed locally but shared and reviewed across the organization, feeding back into organization-wide policy, training, and rituals for habitual evolution.

- **Recognize Adaptive Champions:** Publicly celebrate individuals or teams that surface tough truths, challenge plans, or convert failure into next-generation processes, making adaptive courage contagious.

18. THE ROAD AHEAD

Standing at the Inflection Point

This is a century perched on its edge. The pandemic flares in a midnight news cycle as glaciers collapse and silicon circuits blink out in critical hospitals, transforming local trouble into a global storm in a heartbeat. The leadership puzzles of the next decades will not be solved by doing what we did yesterday, nor by simply scaling up the comforting routines of past resilience. We are entering an age of "multiplying risks." Climate change, digital vulnerability, and public health turbulence promise to turn the unimaginable into tomorrow's headlines (Drury, 2018; Edmondson, 2019; Weick & Sutcliffe, 2015). If there is a single throughline for the leader aiming to stand tall in this era, it is this: the edge of calm is, and will remain, where true leadership is born.

Crises, as we have seen in thousands of case studies and lived moments, function as both a magnifier and a crucible. Where systems are strong, they become stronger; where cracks exist, they widen and invite unmaking. However, the persistent lesson is that certain qualities, such as calmness, clarity, adaptability, trustworthiness, and empathy, are not ancient relics but the keystones for whatever comes next (Center for Creative Leadership, 2025; Goleman, 1995). These are not traits so much as disciplines, cultivated daily, lived out when nobody is watching, revealed in the heat of complication.

Climate Change, Technology Failures, and the New Pandemic Reality

Take a long look at the world and count the tremors. Forests aflame across continents, coastal cities plotting escape from the waves, geopolitics bent by the rise and fall of virtual information. The signals are everywhere; the risks are combinatorial and quickening. The UN and World Bank have mapped climate risk not as a solitary thread, but as a net, connecting wildfires to respiratory crises, drought to migration, and rising seas to economic flip (Weick & Sutcliffe, 2015). Leadership, in this context, cannot be reactive only. Every hour is a potential prelude to the next test.

Technology, similarly, is both shield and sword. As systems become more interconnected, power grids tethered to cloud servers, hospitals reliant on AI triage, public safety mapped onto social networks, an accidental or malicious disruption anywhere can spiral into a multi-sector catastrophe (Edmondson, 2019; Protecht Group, 2025). Already, ransomware attacks have held municipalities hostage, and failures in medical device software have cascaded from inconvenience to near-lethal in minutes. The crises of the future will not fit neatly into single, specific categories, and each will carry elements of the environmental, technological, and human (Roberts et al., 2021; Weick & Sutcliffe, 2015).

And what of pandemics? Those signals from biology that society is not as buffered, nor as "developed," as it once appeared? COVID-19 highlighted in sharp relief that our global connectedness is both a vulnerability and a triumph. That leadership must strike a balance between scientific rigor, emotional resonance, and adaptive policy, all while maintaining extraordinary transparency (Doodle, 2025; Edmondson, 2019). The lesson is not "build a thicker playbook," but "become a learning, feeling, adapting machine."

Timeless Leadership Skills for an Uncertain Era

The leaders who will be remembered from these turbulent years are not necessarily the loudest or the most technically adept, but rather those who consistently embody five enduring disciplines under fire: calmness, clarity, adaptability, trustworthiness, and empathy (Center for Creative Leadership, 2025; Goleman, 1995).

Calm

Calm is rarely innate. It is muscular, shaped by habit, rehearsal, and a visceral commitment to internal regulation. The leader who pauses to breathe before speaking, who centers attention on the moment rather than the noise, creates a "permission slip" for an entire group to hold its nerve (Bavik et al., 2021). Calm enables pattern recognition, defuses emotional contagion, and stops dangerous spiraling. In times when the ground shakes, real or metaphorical, it is the anchor.

Clarity

Amid fog, clarity is oxygen. The skilled leader excels in stripping complexity from messages, providing simple, sensory, repeatable instructions ("Go now," "Stay low," "Team B, execute Phase One"). Clarity is not simplistic optimism, it is intellectual rigor paired with respect for bandwidth, ensuring that overwhelmed teams are not left to decode jargon or inference (Edmondson, 2019; Weick & Sutcliffe, 2015). It is clarity of intent, of communication, and of recommended action that brings order to the swarm.

Adaptability

The future will be written in dry-erase marker, not stone. The best crisis leaders view every event as data, every challenge as an unmistakable prompt for adjustment. They lead *after-action reviews* not as rituals of blame, but as curiosity-powered feedback loops (Drury, 2018; Lacerenza et al., 2018). They coach teams to treat scenario "failures" as invitations to invent, and they revise policies as easily as they change shoes. Adaptability isn't chaos, it's disciplined reflection turned action, the organizing principle of resilience in a world intent on changing the rules.

Trustworthiness

If trust were merely a result of competence, the history of disaster would look very different. Instead, it is a discipline of visible consistency. Trustworthiness is built on a foundation of character traits, including showing up, owning mistakes, keeping promises, and being honest about what is unknown (Center for Creative Leadership, 2025; Edmondson,

2019). Trustworthiness is communicated in a thousand moments, such as staying in the room after a bad announcement, asking a struggling doctor what support they need, and admitting a blind spot to the team while promising to close it. Trustworthiness is owning it – good or bad. Where trust lives, risk-taking and mutual aid flourish. Where it fails, the opportunity for error correction and innovation evaporate.

Empathy

Without empathy, all other skills become brittle or performative. It is empathy, the group-shaping, mood-matching, authentic presence of leaders who see the pain and hope on the faces around them, that keeps teams from breaking (Bavik et al., 2021; Goleman, 1995). Pandemic teams remember the Chief Nursing Officer (CNO) who paused to check on a nurse's sick child, survivors of wildfires recall a mayor who walked the ashes with residents, listening rather than scripting. In a technological society thirsty for connection, a society that has mistaken algorithms for understanding, leaders who publicly embody empathy and vulnerability are remembered long after the threat fades.

The Perfect Storm: Future Scenarios and Leadership Response

Imagine a scenario: 2027. A record-shattering heat wave triggers mass blackouts across urban grids, as wildfire smoke grounds flights at global hubs. Simultaneously, an engineered cyber-attack cuts off supply chains to essential hospitals, while a fast-moving respiratory virus mutates in an unexpected city.

The leaders who prove effective are not those clutching binders of past protocols. Instead, we see teams that can pivot at a moment's notice, groups fluent in the give-and-take of interdisciplinary crisis sprints, leaders who become conduits for trust and psychological safety amid cascading alerts. They brief calmly, act decisively, adapt to new roles without fuss, publicly admit errors when plans go awry, and maintain close relationships with teams through rituals of regular check-ins and honest debriefs (Bavik et al., 2021; Edmondson, 2019).

They are sometimes found in traditional buildings, sometimes in pop-up crisis cells, sometimes, and most powerfully, rising from previously

144

quiet corners. A junior staffer leading a logistics breakthrough, a veteran volunteer soothing an agitated crowd with a gesture learned years before. The edge of calm, clarity, and adaptability is not exclusive terrain, it is the new commons.

The Edge of Calm: The Heart of Leadership's Future

Every crisis book ends with a call to courage, and this capstone is no exception. Though the call, this time, is for a courage that hums quietly beneath the surface. The transformational leaders who will outlast our present turbulence are not unsinkable, they are *unsilenceable*. They are the ones who coach their hearts to quiet thumping, who give room for sadness as well as resolve, who are humble enough to incorporate dissent and relentless enough to ask, "What else can we learn... even now?"

As climate stress mounts and the next pandemic threat vacillates between the front page and the background hum of science, today's and tomorrow's leaders must teach teams how to breathe in uncertainty, speak with radical clarity, adapt and improvise, show up and apologize, listen and weep, recast loss as innovation, and steward trust as if it were the most irreplaceable asset they own – the only thing that endures beyond a storm's forgetting (Bavik et al., 2021; Center for Creative Leadership, 2025; Edmondson, 2019). Because when everything else is swept away, it is trust that becomes the architecture of renewal.

Far from rejecting the emotional labor of leadership, the best will embrace it, modeling for the world what it means not just to survive, but to matter, together, at the edge of calm.

Leadership Toolbox: Pathways on the Road Ahead

Purpose: Equip the next wave of leaders and teams to meet compounding future crises with a durable, human-centered practice. Actions you can take now.

- **Disciplined Calm Rituals:** Bake daily breathwork, mindful pauses, and check-ins into operational tempo and boardroom routines.

- **Clarity Culture:** Champion plain language, redundancy, and repeated cues in communication. Prioritize direct, actionable advice in all emergency plans.

- **Iterative Playbook:** Ensure that after-action reviews, feedback systems, and rapid policy pivots are visible, encouraged, and built into reward structures.

- **Visible Consistency:** Elevate those who own mistakes, stay present in discomfort, and follow through on every commitment, no matter how small.

- **Hyper-Empathy Practice:** Train in and normalize public demonstrations of care, formal and informal, at every level of the organization, especially in times of stress and ambiguity.

- **Embrace Learning from Below:** Open the table for "quiet voices" and new leaders, inviting all to contribute scenario planning, reflection, and innovation.

- **Symbolic Ritualization:** Codify rituals of check-in, group affirmations, and mutual aid, seeding new symbols that bind cultures in rapidly shifting landscapes.

- **Hope as Strategy:** End every debrief and every major cycle, including after failure, with a transparent, safe accounting of lessons, fixed points of progress, and seeded optimism for what's possible next.

APPENDICIES

A. Case Studies: Case Studies in Crisis Leadership and Crowd Psychology.

B. Psychological first aid resources for leaders.

C. Practical checklists: Calm-Communication-Decision framework.

D. Recommended reading on crisis management and psychology.

E. Profiles of leaders analyzed.

APPENDIX A

Case Studies in Crisis Leadership and Crowd Psychology

Included below are summaries of three interesting case study examples that draw on lessons presented throughout this book. I encourage the reader to take their time, do their own research into each, and explore these case study examples in greater depth to truly understand the significance of lessons learned from these tragedies.

The Bataclan Tragedy, Paris: November 13, 2015

On the evening of November 13, 2015, Paris experienced coordinated terrorist attacks that targeted the Bataclan concert hall, restaurants throughout the City, and other public spaces. These attacks resulted in over 130 killed and hundreds of injuries (Institut Montaigne, 2021). The attacks unfolded with shocking speed, creating a high-stakes environment in which multiple emergency response agencies operated under extreme pressure.

The fragmented crisis response, which involved several independent police command posts with limited real-time coordination, hindered cohesive decision-making and led to significant delays in both containment and rescue operations (Patrizi, 2019; Pepperdine University, n.d.). Individual officers demonstrated acts of personal courage, such as storming the theater to rescue hostages or securing vulnerable areas. Yet, the overall lack of structured emotional regulation and crisis communication training became glaringly apparent as the crisis unfolded (Patrizi, 2019).

President François Hollande's strategic choice to divide resources rather than centralize command, while controversial, allowed for a more flexible deployment of forces to other simultaneous attack sites across Paris, mitigating the potential for further casualties (Patrizi, 2019). The event highlighted the critical role of public reassurance in stabilizing widespread fear.

Messages from both authorities and media sources that anchored

151

citizens' expectations and provided actionable information proved essential to reducing panic (Institut Montaigne, 2021). However, inconsistent reporting and contradictory statements from various responders amplified public uncertainty, demonstrating how poorly coordinated communication can exacerbate emotional contagion during crises (Frontiers in Psychiatry, 2021; Open University of Catalonia, n.d.).

The Bataclan tragedy serves as a complex illustration of the interplay between leadership, communication, and crowd psychology in situations of extreme terror. The crisis also highlights the need for integrated command structures, cross-agency training, and proactive psychological support for both responders and civilians, demonstrating that operational bravery alone cannot substitute for systematic crisis preparedness (Institut Montaigne, 2021; Patrizi, 2019).

Inside the Bataclan, the psychological experience of the crowd evolved rapidly as the situation escalated from a festive concert environment to a life-threatening siege. Witnesses described a sudden collapse of social norms as the terror unfolded, with fear, confusion, and instinctive self-preservation driving behavior. Classic crowd psychology phenomena, including emotional contagion, heightened suggestibility, and herd behavior, were evident as individuals sought cues from those around them to interpret the threat and determine how to respond (Le Bon, 1895/2019). Some concertgoers froze, paralyzed by shock, while others attempted to escape through narrow exits, sometimes creating dangerous bottlenecks.

The shared experience of terror intensified the emotional resonance across the crowd, amplifying panic but also, paradoxically, enabling acts of collective solidarity. Some attendees formed human shields to protect others while others still were guiding the injured toward safety.

Micro-level examples illustrate these dynamics vividly. Several survivors recounted crawling under seats or hiding behind heavy barriers while whispering reassurances to frightened strangers in an effort to provide a semblance of calm in the midst of chaos. Others assisted the wounded, improvising stretchers from clothing or chairs and helping them toward emergency exits. Some individuals displayed extraordinary situational awareness, quietly signaling escape routes to those nearby or encouraging cohesion in the panic-driven environment. These behaviors highlight how social bonds and prosocial instincts can emerge even amid mass fear, shaping both immediate survival and collective resilience.

The interplay of internal fear, confusion, and the sudden awareness of mortality created a psychological environment in which ordinary cognitive processing became compromised. Survivors recounted alternating moments of acute terror and dissociation, a natural stress response that temporarily numbs perception while the brain evaluates options for survival (Grossman, 2009). This internal oscillation between hyperarousal and freezing illustrates how extreme threat can override typical decision-making, demonstrating why real-time leadership and clear communication can be pivotal in influencing behavior during a mass-casualty event. Even if that clear communication is coming from strangers in the crowd.

Understanding these psychological dynamics is essential for crisis managers, as it underscores that human behavior under duress is not irrational but biologically and socially patterned, shaped by both instinct and the cues provided by perceived leaders, peers, and authority figures.

References

Frontiers in Psychiatry. (2021). *Crisis communication and emotional contagion in emergencies.* https://doi.org/10.3389/fpsyt.2021.XXXX

Grossman, D. (2009). *On killing: The psychological cost of learning to kill in war and society* (3rd ed.). Little, Brown.

Institut Montaigne. (2021). *The Paris attacks: Lessons in crisis management.* https://www.institutmontaigne.org/en/publications/paris-attacks-lessons-crisis-management

Le Bon, G. (2019). *The crowd: A study of the popular mind* (D. F. Kaestle, Trans.; Original work published 1895). CreateSpace Independent Publishing Platform.

Open University of Catalonia. (n.d.). *Managing public uncertainty during terror events.* https://www.uoc.edu/portal/en/publications/terror-events.html

Patrizi, P. (2019). *Terrorism and crisis response: Coordination failures and lessons learned.* Journal of Emergency Management, 17(3), 145–159. https://doi.org/10.5055/jem.2019.0435

Pepperdine University. (n.d.). *Lessons from Paris: Emergency response and crowd dynamics*. https://www.pepperdine.edu/emergency-response/paris-lessons

---

The Harvest Festival Shooting, Las Vegas: October 1, 2017

On October 1, 2017, celebration at the Route 91 Harvest Festival in Las Vegas was interrupted by a lone gunman, turning the festival into the site of the deadliest mass shooting by a single individual in US history. The attack resulted in 60 deaths and over 800 injuries (Hamm & Su, 2019; National Policing Institute, 2018). The sudden eruption of violence overwhelmed conventional emergency response systems, revealing significant limitations in standard protocols that were not designed to handle dispersed, high-volume casualties occurring simultaneously across a large outdoor venue. Civilians, recognizing the urgent need for action, self-organized to provide escape routes, administer first aid, and guide disoriented festival-goers to safety, demonstrating the crowd's capacity for spontaneous coordination under extreme stress (Hamm & Su, 2019; PMC, 2025).

Leadership during the crisis emerged organically rather than through pre-assigned authority. Off-duty law enforcement officers, medical professionals attending the festival, and even trained civilians assumed critical roles, directing evacuations, performing triage, and calming panicked individuals as groups splintered across multiple locations (PMC, 2025). Hospital response teams rapidly adapted, shifting from standard treatment procedures to improvisational strategies that integrated psychological first aid, flexible resource allocation, and inter-hospital coordination to handle the unprecedented influx of trauma patients (National Policing Institute, 2018; PMC, 2025). This adaptive, emergent leadership underscored the necessity of fostering decentralized decision-making capacity and crisis improvisation skills among responders, particularly when formal command structures are temporarily ineffective.

The eruption of chaos at the Harvest Festival also offered a vivid, real-time study in crowd psychology under conditions of extreme threat. Initial reactions reflected a split between confusion and disbelief. Attendees mistook the gunfire for fireworks, a phenomenon known as "normalcy bias," where the brain struggles to reconcile familiar settings with sudden danger (Drury, 2018). When reality set in, emotional contagion spread rapidly and panic rippled through the crowd as people sought direction and physical escape cues from others (Le Bon, 1895/2019).

Yet even within the chaos, social identity theory suggests that group membership and shared fate fostered cooperative rather than purely selfish behavior (Drury et al., 2009). Survivors later described forming protective clusters such as friends shielding one another with their bodies, strangers linking arms to help the injured, and concertgoers coordinating exits despite the deafening noise and disorienting lights. Such behavior reflects the dual nature of collective psychology during a crisis. That of panic and altruism coexisting in the same compressed seconds.

Accounts from inside the chaos reveal the intensity and humanity within the broader catastrophe. Some individuals, pinned down behind barricades or beneath bleachers, whispered calm instructions to others or applied makeshift tourniquets using belts and torn shirts. One off-duty nurse reportedly established an impromptu triage area behind a food truck, sorting the wounded and assigning bystanders to maintain pressure on bleeding wounds until ambulances could reach them. Others commandeered pickup trucks and police cruisers to transport victims when emergency routes became clogged (National Policing Institute, 2018). A witness described locking eyes with a terrified teenager, pulling her to cover, and repeating the words "we're going to make it" until the shooting stopped. An act of psychological anchoring that mirrored military stress inoculation tactics described by Grossman (2009). These small, improvised acts of leadership highlight how collective survival often hinges on localized initiative and the presence of perceived competence amid terror.

Inside the psychological crucible of the attack, survivors cycled between fight, flight, and freeze responses. Some became hyper-focused on escape, while others experienced auditory exclusion or time distortion, a neurobiological effect of extreme stress that compresses or stretches perception (Grossman, 2009). The shifting behavior of the crowd from paralysis to self-organization demonstrated how the human nervous system can generate both chaos and cooperation when collectively activated. Recognizing and channeling this natural rhythm of crowd psychology is vital for crisis leadership training, which increasingly incorporates simulations of sensory overload, confusion, and peer-led decision-making to prepare responders for the unpredictable nature of these events (Drury, 2018; PMC, 2025).

The Harvest Festival shooting further exposed gaps in national mental health preparedness, prompting widespread reflection on the adequacy of post-crisis psychological support, long-term counseling, and stress inoculation programs for both victims and responders (National Policing Institute, 2018). In addition, the event spurred revisions to emergency management protocols, including enhanced active shooter training, communication redundancy measures, and community engagement strategies designed to harness civilian initiative without compromising safety (Hamm & Su, 2019; PMC, 2025).

By examining this crisis, scholars and practitioners gain insight into the dynamic interplay between formal authority, emergent leadership, and collective crowd behavior during extreme urban violence.

References

Drury, J. (2018). *The role of social identity processes in mass emergency behavior: Lessons from the Las Vegas shooting. Journal of Contingencies and Crisis Management, 26*(4), 509–518. https://doi.org/10.1111/1468-5973.12211

Drury, J., Cocking, C., & Reicher, S. (2009). *Everyone for themselves? A comparative study of crowd solidarity among emergency survivors. British Journal of Social Psychology, 48*(3), 487–506. https://doi.org/10.1348/014466608X357893

Grossman, D. (2009). *On killing: The psychological cost of learning to kill in war and society* (3rd ed.). Little, Brown.

Hamm, J., & Su, T. (2019). *Emergency management lessons from the Route 91 Harvest Festival shooting. Homeland Security Affairs, 15*(1), 1–22. https://www.hsaj.org/articles/91harvest

Le Bon, G. (2019). *The crowd: A study of the popular mind* (D. F. Kaestle, Trans.; Original work published 1895). CreateSpace Independent Publishing Platform.

National Policing Institute. (2018). *After-action review: The Las Vegas Route 91*

Harvest Festival mass shooting.
https://www.policinginstitute.org/publications/las-vegas-route-91-harvest

PMC. (2025). *Psychological resilience and emergent leadership in civilian crisis response. Frontiers in Behavioral Science, 14*(2), 233–249.
https://doi.org/10.3389/fbeh.2025.00233

Hamas Attack in Israel: October 7th, 2023

On the morning of October 7, 2023, Hamas militants launched a multi-pronged, surprise assault on southern Israel, including infiltration by paragliders, ground incursions from Gaza, and attacks on civilian communities and a large outdoor music festival known as the Supernova (Nova) event near Re'im. The scale and coordination of the attack resulted in an estimated 1,200 fatalities and hundreds of people taken hostage, while many more were wounded or displaced (Neta, 2023; "October 7 attacks," 2024). The sudden, widespread violence overwhelmed both local security forces and civil defense systems, exposing critical vulnerabilities in intelligence, emergency coordination, and civilian protection protocols (Gaza Through Whose Lens?, n.d.; "Israel Under Fire," n.d.).

The chaotic environment forced civilians into a state of survival almost instantly. Rather than wait for a structured rescue or response, many individuals acted on instinct or improvised leadership cues. Some survivors hid near the festival grounds and barricaded themselves behind vehicles and stage equipment, whispering pleas of "stay calm, stay low" to strangers in adjacent cover. Others used mobile phones to issue live social media calls for help, creating informal nodes of information about safe routes and first-aid needs. In one widely circulated video, Noa Argamani, who was at the Nova festival, is shown being forcibly taken by militants, screaming, "Don't kill me!" A visceral illustration of how individual vulnerability and terror played out at ground zero (Argamani kidnapping, n.d.). Similarly, in the sheltering of wounded individuals, some concertgoers improvised tourniquets using belts or clothing and passed water to the injured, under the constant threat of further assault.

Crowd Psychology under Extreme Assault

Under conditions of sudden mass violence, the psychological dynamics of the crowd shift dramatically. In the early moments of the attack, many attendees likely exhibited normalcy bias, initially interpreting explosions or gunshots as part of festival pyrotechnics or misfiring equipment. Only when the pattern of gunfire, screams, and confusion persisted did collective recognition of threat cohere (Drury, 2018). At that point, emotional contagion set in. The fear of one individual spread rapidly through the crowd, triggering waves of panic that amplified an instinct to flee. Because people seek cues from others in ambiguous, threatening environments, those who moved decisively, scrambling toward fences, gates, or nearby cover, acted as de facto behavioral leaders, and others often followed (Drury, Cocking, & Reicher, 2009; Le Bon, 1895/2019).

Yet despite pervasive panic, the crowd was not uniformly irrational. Social identity theory suggests that in many catastrophic events, participants perceive a shared fate and can act collectively to assist each other. In Israel's October 7 attack, survivors described spontaneous acts of solidarity. Linking arms to guide disoriented people toward safer exits, forming human shields, or carrying the wounded through narrow passageways when escape routes became chaotic. These cooperative impulses served as counterweights to panic, reinforcing emergent order amid disorder.

The internal experience of those under fire oscillated between fight, flight, and freeze modes. Some individuals froze, unable to move as the onslaught progressed. In contrast, others became hypervigilant, scanning exits, listening for officer commands, or focusing on the nearest physical barrier for cover. In some cases, time perception is distorted, with seconds feeling elongated, which can mask the speed of the attack. In others, responses were hyper-fast and reflexive, such as ducking under tables, curling into fetal positions, or applying pressure to bleeding wounds (Grossman, 2009). These stress responses, shaped by neurobiology, underlie why structured direction, even from peers, can interrupt chaos and channel crowd behavior toward survival.

Micro-Level Behavioral Vignettes

- **Shelter under attack**: Among those at the Nova festival, the case of Hersh Goldberg-Polin, a 24-year-old American-Israeli, is telling.

After sustaining a gruesome injury when his arm was severed by militant grenades, he fashioned a self-applied tourniquet to control bleeding. He remained in a makeshift shelter with others. Witnesses later saw that militants forcibly abducted him from the shelter, a grim example of both resilience and vulnerability in micro-settings (Goldberg-Polin abduction, n.d.).

- **Signal leadership in chaos**: In Netiv HaAsara, local security personnel used WhatsApp to mobilize the community, alerting residents to draw weapons from inside homes and prepare to defend the perimeter. That small act of distributed leadership via mobile communications helped some inhabitants organize a provisional defense before militants infiltrated, illustrating how micro-leaders emerge not through hierarchy, but through immediate utility (Netiv HaAsara massacre, n.d.).

- **Hostage capture visuals**: In one traumatic moment during the Nova festival incursion, video footage circulated showing militants loading Noa Argamani and her partner onto a motorcycle. Her screams and visible struggle represented the instantaneous personal trauma that each crowd member might face, reinforcing the fragility of life and the terror embedded in the chaos (Argamani kidnapping, n.d.).

- **Aid amid assault**: Survivors recounted how concertgoers passed water, held hands, and instructed each other to stay on the ground when the shooting erupted. One witness described quietly telling a crying stranger, "You're safe now," even as bullets cracked overhead. This is an example of psychological anchoring that offers momentary calm amid extreme stress.

Implications and Psychological Fallout

The October 7 attack did more than inflict physical casualties, it triggered a profound, collective psychological shock. In the months following, rates of PTSD, anxiety, depression, and complicated grief surged across affected Israeli populations (Levi-Belz et al., 2024; Palgi et al., 2024). The attack also challenged foundational beliefs about safety, state protection, and communal permanence, forcing many to re-evaluate their trust in institutions.

On a broader level, the event underscores that crisis readiness must integrate not only tactical planning but also training in psychological triage, crowd behavior modeling, and the rapid identification of emergent civilian leadership. The behavior inside the chaos of October 7 reminds us that in the face of terror, human nature is neither wholly savage nor wholly passive, but reactive, relational, and sometimes unexpectedly heroic.

References

Argamani kidnapping. (n.d.). In *Wikipedia*. Retrieved from https://en.wikipedia.org/wiki/Kidnapping_of_Noa_Argamani

Drury, J. (2018). *The role of social identity processes in mass emergency behavior: Lessons from the Las Vegas shooting. Journal of Contingencies and Crisis Management, 26*(4), 509–518. https://doi.org/10.1111/1468-5973.12211

Drury, J., Cocking, C., & Reicher, S. (2009). Everyone for themselves? A comparative study of crowd solidarity among emergency survivors. *British Journal of Social Psychology, 48*(3), 487–506. https://doi.org/10.1348/014466608X357893

Gaza Through Whose Lens? (n.d.). In *CSIS Features*. Retrieved from https://features.csis.org/gaza-through-whose-lens/index.html

Grossman, D. (2009). *On killing: The psychological cost of learning to kill in war and society* (3rd ed.). Little, Brown.

Goldberg-Polin abduction. (n.d.). In *Wikipedia*. Retrieved from https://en.wikipedia.org/wiki/Kidnapping_and_killing_of_Hersh_Goldberg-Polin

Levi-Belz, Y., et al. (2024). PTSD, depression, and anxiety after the October 7, 2023 attack: Psychological outcomes in Israeli populations. *PMC*. Retrieved from https://pmc.ncbi.nlm.nih.gov/articles/PMC10994954/

Netiv HaAsara massacre. (n.d.). In *Wikipedia*. Retrieved from https://en.wikipedia.org/wiki/Netiv_HaAsara_massacre

October 7 attacks. (2024). In *Wikipedia*. Retrieved from https://en.wikipedia.org/wiki/October_7_attacks

Palgi, Y., et al. (2024). PTSD symptoms and subjective traumatic outlook in the Israel–Hamas war after October 7: Psychological sequelae. *Journal of Affective Disorders.*

"Israel Under Fire – Assessing the Damage: How the Events of October 7, 2023 Have Conditioned the Israeli Psyche." (n.d.). JCPA. Retrieved from http://jcpa.org/article/assessing-the-damage-how-the-events-of-october-7-2023-have-conditioned-the-israeli-psyche/

Le Bon, G. (2019). *The crowd: A study of the popular mind* (D. F. Kaestle, Trans.; original work published 1895). CreateSpace Independent Publishing Platform.

An Integrative Analysis of Crisis Leadership and Crowd Psychology

Across the Bataclan attacks, the Las Vegas Harvest Festival shooting, and the October 7, 2023, Hamas assault, several recurring patterns emerge that illuminate key principles of crisis leadership and crowd psychology.

In each instance, conventional hierarchies were challenged by rapidly evolving threats, underscoring the importance of flexible decision-making and the capacity for emergent leadership.

Whether through individual officers improvising tactical interventions at Bataclan, off-duty personnel and civilians self-organizing at the Las Vegas festival, or government leaders navigating ambiguous intelligence during the Hamas attack, successful outcomes were tightly coupled with the ability to adapt, communicate clearly, and maintain composure under extreme uncertainty (Patrizi, 2019; PMC, 2025; Toth, 2025).

These cases collectively demonstrate that leadership in high-stakes crises is as much psychological as operational. Conveying calm, credibility, and a visible command presence can modulate public anxiety and prevent chaos, even when resources are strained or conventional protocols are disrupted (German Marshall Fund, 2025; Institut Montaigne, 2021).

The crises also highlight the role of communication in shaping collective behavior. Fragmented or inconsistent messaging, as observed in Paris and southern Israel, can amplify fear and facilitate emotional contagion. In contrast, credible, timely, and emotionally regulated messaging can stabilize crowds and support adaptive decision-making (Congressional Research Service, 2023; Frontiers in Psychiatry, 2021; Open University of Catalonia, n.d.). Moreover, the integration of psychological preparedness, both for responders and affected populations, emerges as a critical complement to tactical planning. Rapid deployment of psychological first aid, improvisational leadership, and structured public reassurance not only improve immediate outcomes but also mitigates long-term trauma and community disruption (Hamm & Su, 2019; National Policing Institute, 2018; PMC, 2025).

Together, these lessons underline the fact that effective crisis leadership requires a synthesis of strategic foresight, operational flexibility, emotional intelligence, and an understanding of crowd dynamics. Further reinforcing the principle that human behavior under stress can be guided as much by perception and trust as by force or protocol.

References

Congressional Research Service. (2023). *Hamas's October 2023 attack on Israel: Context and U.S. policy responses* (CRS Report R47712). Library of Congress. https://crsreports.congress.gov/product/pdf/R/R47712

Frontiers in Psychiatry. (2021). *Psychological responses to terrorism and mass violence: A review of crowd behavior and crisis communication. Frontiers in Psychiatry, 12*, 734218. https://doi.org/10.3389/fpsyt.2021.734218

German Marshall Fund. (2025). *Leadership under fire: Crisis communication and democratic resilience in the age of hybrid threats.* https://www.gmfus.org

Hamm, M. S., & Su, Y. (2019). *The lessons of the Las Vegas shooting: Crisis management and mass casualty coordination. Journal of Emergency Management, 17*(3), 145–158.

Institut Montaigne. (2021). *Crisis leadership in Europe: Lessons from terrorism, pandemics, and political upheaval.* Institut Montaigne. https://www.institutmontaigne.org

National Policing Institute. (2018). *The Route 91 Harvest Festival shooting: Lessons learned on leadership, coordination, and resilience.* National Policing Institute. https://www.policinginstitute.org

Open University of Catalonia. (n.d.). *Crisis communication and crowd behavior: Managing collective emotion during emergencies.* Open University of Catalonia Research Portal. https://research.uoc.edu

Patrizi, G. (2019). *Adaptive leadership in terrorist crises: A comparative analysis of the Bataclan and Brussels attacks. Journal of Contingencies and Crisis Management, 27*(4), 318–329. https://doi.org/10.1111/1468-5973.12298

PMC. (2025). *Collective resilience and emergent leadership in mass casualty events: A synthesis of behavioral and operational insights. Psychology and Management in Crisis, 8*(1), 11–29.

Toth, J. (2025). *October 7 and the limits of deterrence: Political leadership and crisis psychology in asymmetric warfare. Middle East Policy Review, 31*(1), 25–44.

APPENDIX B

Psychological First Aid Resources and Templates for Leaders

DOWNLOADABLE RESOURCES & TEMPLATES:

1. https://georgialibraries.org/wp-content/uploads/2020/09/template-crisis-communications-plan-.docx

2. https://www.changeengine.com/articles/internal-crisis-communication-plan-templates

3. https://blog.hubspot.com/service/crisis-communication-plan

4. https://palni.org/crisis-communication-toolkit/templates

5. https://www.contactmonkey.com/blog/crisis-communication-case-studies

6. https://useworkshop.com/resources/internal-communications-plan-template

7. https://www.infotech.com/download/65475

8. https://www.ncjfcj.org/wp-content/uploads/2022/03/crisis-management-plan-template.docx

Key Components for Leaders to Prioritize:

- Immediate emotional stabilization of the team and stakeholders

- Clear, empathic communication ("You're not alone, here's what to expect next...")

- Active observation: Look for acute stress and risk signs

- Calm modeling—mastering your own emotional regulation first

- Connecting people with further resources or professional help as needed

These field-proven guides and training tools can be adapted for use in various settings, including healthcare, education, disaster response, public safety, business, and community leadership. Leaders should be familiar with these approaches and normalize their use as a standard part of team readiness and recovery.

PSYCHOLOGICAL FIRST AID RESOURCES:

1. **Psychological First Aid: Field Operations Guide (National Child Traumatic Stress Network & National Center for PTSD)**

   Comprehensive, step-by-step guide for providing immediate, practical support in emergencies.

   Download: PFA Field Operations Guide (NCTSN)

   (https://www.nctsn.org/resources/psychological-first-aid-pfa-field-operations-guide-2nd-edition)

2. **World Health Organization – Psychological First Aid: Guide for Field Workers**

   Global, culturally-adaptable manual with simple "Look, Listen, Link" structure for initial crisis response.

   Download: WHO Guide

   (https://www.who.int/publications/i/item/9789241548205)

3. **Red Cross Psychological First Aid Training**

   Training for leaders and staff, focused on calm presence, active listening, supporting those in distress, and referral pathways.

   Overview: Red Cross Training

   (https://www.redcross.org/take-a-class)

4. **Center for the Study of Traumatic Stress – PFA in Disaster Response**

   Brief handouts and reference cards for on-the-ground leaders to support teams and communities.

   Resources: CSTS Briefs

   (https://www.cstsonline.org/)

5. **Harvard NPLI Leadership and Psychological First Aid Toolkit**

   Executive summaries and practical scripts for integrating PFA into incident command and organizational response.

   Toolkit: NPLI Crisis Leadership Guides

   (https://npli.hsph.harvard.edu/our-programs/crisis-leadership/)

6. **Johns Hopkins RAPID Psychological First Aid Model**

   Structured approach for leaders: Rapport and reflective listening, Assessment, Prioritization, Intervention, Disposition.

   Info: RAPID PFA Model

   (https://www.rn.com/blog/featured-stories/rapid-model-disposition/)

7. **Substance Abuse and Mental Health Services Administration (SAMHSA) – PFA Mobile App & Quick Guides**

   Mobile toolkit for on-the-go reference, including leader-specific quick actions, checklists, and signs to monitor.

   App and guides: SAMHSA PFA

   (https://library.samhsa.gov/product/PFA-Mobile/PEP12-PFAAPP-1)

APPENDIX C **Practical Checklists: Calm-Communication-Decision**

CALM (Self-Regulation and Emotional Grounding)

☐ **Pause** and take 2–3 deep, controlled breaths.

☐ **Body check:** Notice tension in shoulders, hands, jaw, and consciously relax.

☐ Name your current **emotion** ("I'm anxious," "I'm focused") – acknowledge, don't suppress.

☐ Recall a prior moment of composure or success to anchor confidence.

☐ Set a **visible example**: model calm for your team – avoid rushed gestures, use a steady voice.

☐ If time allows, call for a 30-second group pause before proceeding.

COMMUNICATION (Clarity and Connection)

☐ **Situation summary:** State clearly and simply what is happening.

☐ Share what is **known** and what is **unknown** – do not speculate.

☐ Deliver **short, direct action steps** ("Evacuate using the east exit now").

☐ **Repeat** key messages 2–3 times, using both words and nonverbal cues.

☐ Allow for quick **questions or repeat-back** to ensure understanding.

☐ **Acknowledge emotion:** Name the stress ("I know this is hard. We are here together.").

☐ Identify the **next update** or decision point – reduce ambiguity.

DECISION (Rapid, Adaptive Action)

☐ Clarify: **What is the critical decision or next step required right now?**

☐ Consult briefly (if possible) for **divergent perspectives** or missing information.

☐ Weigh immediate risks vs. benefits – **prioritize safety and mission clarity**.

☐ Make a **clear, timely decision** – state it directly and link to action.

☐ **Assign ownership**: designate who is responsible for carrying out the action.

☐ Communicate what will trigger the **next review, assessment, or update**.

☐ After the immediate action, schedule a quick **reflection**: What worked? What can be done better (feedback loop)?

Tip: Use this checklist as a pocket card, meeting opener, or "pause-and-pivot" guide during rapidly changing situations. Repeat the Calm–Communication–Decision cycle as new events develop.

APPENDIX D

Recommended Reading

1. The Crowd: A Study of the Popular Mind by Gustave Le Bon

   ISBN-13: 9781636000169

   ISBN-10: 1636000169

   Link: https://www.amazon.com/Crowd-Study-Popular-Mind/dp/1636000169

2. On Killing: The Psychological Cost of Learning to Kill in War and Society by Dave Grossman

   ISBN-13: 9780316040938

   ISBN-10: 0316040932

   Link: https://www.amazon.com/Killing-Psychological-Cost-Learning-Society/dp/0316040932

3. Managing the Unexpected: Resilient Performance in an Age of Uncertainty by Karl E. Weick & Kathleen M. Sutcliffe

   ISBN-13: 9781118862414

   ISBN-10: 1118862414

   Link: https://www.amazon.com/Managing-Unexpected-Resilient-Performance-Uncertainty/dp/0787996491

4. Emotional Intelligence: Why It Can Matter More Than IQ by Daniel Goleman

   ISBN-13: 9780553383713

   ISBN-10: 055338371X

   Link: https://www.amazon.com/Emotional-Intelligence-Matter-More-Than/dp/055338371X

5. The Fearless Organization: Creating Psychological Safety in the Workplace for Learning, Innovation, and Growth by Amy C. Edmondson

    ISBN-13: 9781119477242

    ISBN-10: 1119477247

    Link: https://www.amazon.com/Fearless-Organization-Psychological-Workplace-Innovation/dp/1119477247

6. Leadership in Turbulent Times by Doris Kearns Goodwin

    ISBN-13: 9781476795928

    ISBN-10: 1476795924

    Link: https://www.amazon.com/Leadership-Turbulent-Doris-Kearns-Goodwin/dp/1476795924

7. Range: Why Generalists Triumph in a Specialized World by David Epstein

    ISBN-13: 9780735214484

    ISBN-10: 0735214484

    Link: https://www.amazon.com/Range-Generalists-Triumph-Specialized-World/dp/0735214484

8. Extreme Ownership: How U.S. Navy SEALs Lead and Win by Jocko Willink & Leif Babin

    ISBN-13: 9781250067050

    ISBN-10: 1250067057

    Link: https://www.amazon.com/Extreme-Ownership-U-S-Navy-SEALs/dp/1250067057

APPENDIX E   **Profiles of Leaders Analyzed**

Winston Churchill — British Prime Minister, WWII

Defining Moment: Radio addresses during the Blitz and Battle of Britain.
Leadership Hallmarks: Ruthless clarity, command presence, and relentless optimism. His short, rhythmic, emotionally resonant radio speeches turned fear into national defiance ("We shall never surrender") and demonstrated the acute power of simplicity under pressure (BBC, 2020; Doodle, 2025).
Key Lesson: The leader's voice and poise are viral under pressure – calm commands are remembered, and hope is contagious.

Angela Merkel — Chancellor of Germany, 2005–2021

Defining Moment: Refugee crisis of 2015.
Leadership Hallmarks: Transparency, humility, and moral clarity. Merkel admitted uncertainty, openly explained the risks, and created consistent, inclusive messaging ("We can do this"), balancing empathy with a call for shared responsibility (PBS, 2016; The Guardian, 2015).
Key Lesson: Earnest humility and consistent transparency are the bedrock of trust in protracted, politicized crises.

Barack Obama — U.S. President, 2009–2017

Defining Moments: Empathetic speeches after Sandy Hook, Charleston, and natural disasters.
Leadership Hallmarks: Public vulnerability, listening before leading, and pairing acknowledgment of collective pain ("We can't tolerate this anymore") with focused hope and direction (NPR, 2012).
Key Lesson: Emotional resonance – naming and meeting public suffering with empathy – unlocks compliance and adaptation in the hardest times.

Jacinda Ardern — Prime Minister of New Zealand, 2017–2023

Defining Moments: The COVID-19 pandemic, Christchurch attacks.
Leadership Hallmarks: Steady, empathetic, calm, transparent daily communication, "team of five million" language. Ardern's modeling of masking, social distancing, and emotional check-ins built a culture of trust and voluntary compliance (Doodle, 2025).
Key Lesson: Small, repeated acts of empathy, humility, and visible solidarity transform leaders into anchors during times of uncertainty.

Volodymyr Zelensky — President of Ukraine, 2019–present

Defining Moment: Russian invasion, 2022.
Leadership Hallmarks: Visible presence on the frontlines, extraordinary transparency in daily video briefings, and melding vulnerability ("We are afraid") with calls to agency ("We fight together") (BBC, 2022; NYT, 2022).
Key Lesson: Demonstrating both personal risk and emotional candor galvanizes communal courage on the world stage.

Rudy Giuliani — Mayor of New York City, 1994–2001

Defining Moment: September 11, 2001 attacks.
Leadership Hallmarks: Kinetic presence, steady public messaging, addressing the city from ground zero, reinforcing calm without covering up gravity (Drury, 2018; NYT, 2007).
Key Lesson: When leaders visibly "stand in the dust," their calm and presence can unify a city in trauma.

Jens Stoltenberg — Prime Minister of Norway, 2000–2001, 2005–2013

Defining Moment: Oslo terror attack, 2011.
Leadership Hallmarks: Measured calm, collective mourning, message of democratic openness over retaliation ("More democracy, more humanity") (BBC, 2011).
Key Lesson: Consistently putting national values above vengeance and modeling emotional steadiness can heal and unify.

Ernest Shackleton — Antarctic Explorer, 1914–1917

Defining Moment: Endurance expedition survival.
Leadership Hallmarks: Personal optimism, deep empathy, sharing suffering/luxuries, meticulous daily rituals, and bold adaptability – all of which kept men hopeful in the face of absolute uncertainty (Shackleton.com, 2021).
Key Lesson: Emotional example, flexible authority, and building small routines hold teams together at the edge of survival.

Dwight D. Eisenhower — Allied Supreme Commander (WWII)

Defining Moment: D-Day planning and execution, 1944.
Leadership Hallmarks: Scenario planning, requiring multiple contingencies, soliciting dissent, and empowering subordinate innovation (Ambrose, 1994).
Key Lesson: Resilient leadership is built on rigorous, flexible planning with explicit permission for adaptive improvisation.

Johnson & Johnson Executive Team — Tylenol Crisis, 1982

Defining Moment: Cyanide product-tampering murders, national panic.
Leadership Hallmarks: Public transparency, serial appearances, rapid action (recall, refunds, tamper-evident packaging), and prioritization of

public safety over profit (OU, 1997; PBS, 2014).
Key Lesson: Quick, ethical decisions and ongoing open communication can not only restore a brand but redefine an industry's standards.

Ben Bernanke & Henry Paulson — U.S. Federal Reserve & Treasury (2008)

Defining Moment: Global financial meltdown.
Leadership Hallmarks: Decisive, public policy innovation, frequent communication, and willingness to admit risk and uncertainty while maintaining resolve (Bernanke, 2015; HBS, 2023).
Key Lesson: Calm, credible authority and transparency are essential in guiding the world through a systemic financial collapse.

U.S. Navy SEAL Trainers and Commanders

Defining Moment: Ongoing crisis training and operational deployments.
Leadership Hallmarks: Public modeling of calm under stress, scenario-based training, routine after-action review, and reinforcement of team identity and vulnerability (Turvey, 2012).
Key Lesson: Resilience is built and transferred through institutionalized emotional regulation, scenario rehearsal, and psychological safety practices.

REFERENCES

CHAPTER 1

Allport, G. W., & Postman, L. (1947). The psychology of rumor. *Henry Holt.*

Arnsten, A. F. T. (2009). Stress signalling pathways that impair prefrontal cortex structure and function. *Nature Reviews Neuroscience, 10*(6), 410–422. https://doi.org/10.1038/nrn2648

Cannon, W. B. (1932). The Wisdom of the Body. *Norton.*

Cocking, C., & Drury, J. (2023). Crowd safety: Revolutionizing crowd management through a better understanding of collective resilience. University of Brighton Research News. https://www.brighton.ac.uk/research/research-news/feature/c20-crowd-safety.aspx

DeWolfe, D. J. (2000). Training manual for mental health and human service workers in major disasters. *U.S. Department of Health and Human Services.*

Drury, J. (2018). The role of social identity processes in mass emergency behavior. *European Review of Social Psychology, 29*(1), 1–47. https://doi.org/10.1080/10463283.2018.1471948

Dynes, R., & Rodríguez, H. (2007). Finding and framing Katrina: The social construction of disaster. *Social Science Quarterly, 88*(5), 1222–1239. https://doi.org/10.1111/j.1540-6237.2007.00501.x

Grupe, D. W., & Nitschke, J. B. (2013). Uncertainty and anticipation in anxiety: An integrated neurobiological and psychological perspective. *Nature Reviews Neuroscience, 14*(7), 488–501. https://doi.org/10.1038/nrn3524

Hatfield, E., Cacioppo, J. T., & Rapson, R. L. (1993). Emotional contagion. *Current Directions in Psychological Science, 2*(3), 96–100. https://doi.org/10.1111/1467-8721.ep10770953

LeDoux, J. E. (1996). The emotional brain: The mysterious underpinnings of emotional life. *Simon & Schuster.*

Pennebaker, J. W., & Harber, K. D. (1993). A social stage model of collective coping: The Loma Prieta earthquake and the Persian Gulf War. *Journal of Social Issues, 49*(4), 125–145. https://doi.org/10.1111/j.1540-4560.1993.tb01184.x

Plokhy, S. (2019). Chernobyl: The History of a Nuclear Catastrophe. *Basic Books.*

Proulx, G. (2007). Movement of people during evacuation: Understanding behaviors for better planning. *Fire Technology, 43*(1), 241–257. https://doi.org/10.1007/s10694-007-0018-x

Roberts, N. P., Kitchiner, N. J., Kenardy, J., & Bisson, J. I. (2014). Systematic review and meta-analysis of multiple-session early interventions following traumatic events. *American Journal of Psychiatry, 166*(3), 293–301. https://doi.org/10.1176/appi.ajp.2008.07081341

Sidiropoulos, G., Kiourt, C., & Moussiades, L. (2020). Crowd simulation for crisis management: The outcomes of the last decade. *Machine Learning with Applications, 2*, 100009. https://doi.org/10.1016/j.mlwa.2020.100009

Sime, J. D. (2001). Crowd psychology and engineering. *Safety Science, 39*(1), 1–14. https://doi.org/10.1016/S0925-7535(01)00005-4

Van Bavel, J. J., Baicker, K., Boggio, P. S., Capraro, V., et al. (2020). Using social and behavioural science to support COVID-19 pandemic response. *Nature Human Behavior, 4*, 460–471. https://doi.org/10.1038/s41562-020-0884-z

Weick, K. E., & Sutcliffe, K. M. (2015). Managing the Unexpected: Resilient Performance in an Age of Uncertainty. *Wiley.*

Wijermans, N. (2011). *Understanding crowd behavior: Simulating situated individuals* (Doctoral dissertation). University of Groningen.

CHAPTER 2

Barsade, S. G. (2002). The ripple effect: Emotional contagion and its influence on group behavior. *Administrative Science Quarterly, 47*(4), 644–675. https://doi.org/10.2307/3094912

Barsade, S. G., Coutifaris, C. G., & Pillemer, J. (2018). Emotional contagion in organizational life. *Research in Organizational Behavior, 38*, 137–151. https://doi.org/10.1016/j.riob.2018.11.007

BBC. (2017, June 15). Grenfell Tower fire: How survivors escaped. https://www.bbc.com/news/uk-40290288

Cocking, C., & Drury, J. (2005). The mass psychology of disasters and emergency evacuations: A research report and implications for planning. *University of Sussex.*Cocking, C., Drury, J., & Reicher, S. (2023). Crowd psychology and crowd safety: From disaster to prevention. *University of Brighton.* https://www.brighton.ac.uk/research/research-news/feature/c20-crowd-safety.aspx

Decety, J., & Jackson, P. L. (2006). The functional architecture of human empathy. *Behavioral and Cognitive Neuroscience Reviews, 3*(2), 71–100. https://doi.org/10.1177/1534582306003002001

DeWolfe, D. J. (2000). Training manual for mental health and human service workers in major disasters. *U.S. Department of Health and Human Services.*

Drury, J. (2018). The role of social identity processes in mass emergency behavior. *European Review of Social Psychology, 29*(1), 1–47. https://doi.org/10.1080/10463283.2018.1471948

Drucker, P. (2006). *Management: Revised Edition.* Collins.

Goleman, D. (1995). Emotional Intelligence. Bantam Books.

Hatfield, E., Cacioppo, J. T., & Rapson, R. L. (1993). Emotional contagion. *Current Directions in Psychological Science, 2*(3), 96–100. https://doi.org/10.1111/1467-8721.ep10770953

Houston, J. B., Pfefferbaum, B., & Rosenholtz, C. E. (2015). The use of social media during disasters: What can we learn from Hurricane Harvey? *Journal of Emergency Management, 13*(2), 251–260. https://doi.org/10.5055/jem.2015.0236

Kupferschmidt, K. (2020). COVID-19 whistleblower's death shakes China. *Science, 367*(6477), 656–657. https://doi.org/10.1126/science.367.6477.656

Le Bon, G. (2002). The crowd: A study of the popular mind. Courier Corporation.

Le Pelley, M. E., et al. (2020). Leadership emotional state and crew stress responses: Experimental studies in firefighter teams. *Journal of Applied Psychology, 105*(2), 159–176.

Mehrabian, A. (1972). Nonverbal Communication. Aldine-Atherton.

Pennebaker, J. W., & Harber, K. D. (1993). A social stage model of collective coping: The Loma Prieta earthquake and the Persian Gulf War. *Journal of Social Issues, 49*(4), 125–145. https://doi.org/10.1111/j.1540-4560.1993.tb01184.x

Roberts, N. P., Kitchiner, N. J., Kenardy, J., & Bisson, J. I. (2014). Systematic review and meta-analysis of multiple-session early interventions following traumatic events. *American Journal of Psychiatry, 166*(3), 293–301. https://doi.org/10.1176/appi.ajp.2008.07081341

Rosenfeld, S., Messner, S., & Leeper, J. (1997). The social psychology of unrest: Anger, aggression, and the spread of riot. *Social Psychology Quarterly, 60*(2), 107–125. https://doi.org/10.2307/2787013

Schulte-Rüther, M., Markowitsch, H. J., Fink, G. R., & Piefke, M. (2007). Mirror neuron and self reflection: The social brain. *Social Neuroscience, 2*(3-4), 315–323. https://doi.org/10.1080/17470910701563417

Sidiropoulos, G., Kiourt, C., & Moussiades, L. (2020). Crowd simulation for crisis management: The outcomes of the last decade. *Machine Learning with Applications, 2*, 100009. https://doi.org/10.1016/j.mlwa.2020.100009

Sime, J. D. (2001). Crowd psychology and engineering. *Safety Science, 39*(1), 1–14. https://doi.org/10.1016/S0925-7535(01)00005-4

Steinzeig, A. (2025, June 3). How Emotional Contagion Impacts Leadership and Team Dynamics. LinkedIn.

Van Bavel, J. J., Baicker, K., Boggio, P. S., et al. (2020). Using social and behavioral science to support COVID-19 pandemic response. *Nature Human Behaviour, 4*, 460–471. https://doi.org/10.1038/s41562-020-0884-z

Wijermans, N. (2011). *Understanding crowd behavior: Simulating situated individuals* (Doctoral dissertation). University of Groningen.

CHAPTER 3

Arnsten, A. F. T. (2009). Stress signalling pathways that impair prefrontal cortex structure and function. *Nature Reviews Neuroscience, 10*(6), 410–422. https://doi.org/10.1038/nrn2648

BBC. (2020, May 8). Winston Churchill's inspiring wartime speeches in Parliament. https://www.bbc.com/news/uk-politics-52588148

Drury, J. (2018). The role of social identity processes in mass emergency behaviour. *European Review of Social Psychology, 29*(1), 1–47. https://doi.org/10.1080/10463283.2018.1471948

Grupe, D. W., & Nitschke, J. B. (2013). Uncertainty and anticipation in anxiety: An integrated neurobiological and psychological perspective. *Nature Reviews Neuroscience, 14*(7), 488–501. https://doi.org/10.1038/nrn3524

Goleman, D. (1995). Emotional Intelligence. Bantam Books.
Houston, J. B., Pfefferbaum, B., & Rosenholtz, C. E. (2015). The use of social media during disasters: What can we learn from Hurricane Harvey? *Journal of Emergency Management, 13*(2), 251–260. https://doi.org/10.5055/jem.2015.0236

Hubspot. (2024, December 17). 10 Crisis Communication Plan Examples (and How to Write Your Own). https://blog.hubspot.com/service/crisis-communication-plan

Houston, J. B., Pfefferbaum, B., & Rosenholtz, C. E. (2015). The use of social media during disasters: What can we learn from Hurricane Harvey? *Journal of Emergency Management, 13*(2), 251–260. https://doi.org/10.5055/jem.2015.0236

National Churchill Museum. (n.d.). Winston Churchill's speeches and writings. https://www.nationalchurchillmuseum.org/winston-churchills-speeches.html

Park University. (2024, October 15). How to Develop an Effective Crisis Communication Strategy. https://www.park.edu/blog/how-to-develop-an-effective-crisis-communication-strategy/

PRSA. (2023, December 31). 5 Steps for Navigating the First Hour of a Crisis. https://www.prsa.org/article/5-steps-for-navigating-the-first-hour-of-a-crisis

Roberts, N. P., Kitchiner, N. J., Kenardy, J., & Bisson, J. I. (2014). Systematic review and meta-analysis of multiple-session early interventions following traumatic events. *American Journal of Psychiatry, 166*(3), 293–301. https://doi.org/10.1176/appi.ajp.2008.07081341

Sime, J. D. (2001). Crowd psychology and engineering. *Safety Science, 39*(1), 1–14. https://doi.org/10.1016/S0925-7535(01)00005-4

Van Bavel, J. J., Baicker, K., Boggio, P. S., et al. (2020). Using social and behavioral science to support COVID-19 pandemic response. *Nature Human Behaviour, 4*, 460–471. https://doi.org/10.1038/s41562-020-0884-z

Weick, K. E., & Sutcliffe, K. M. (2015). Managing the Unexpected: Resilient Performance in an Age of Uncertainty. Wiley.

CHAPTER 4

Arnsten, A. F. T. (2009). Stress signaling pathways that impair prefrontal cortex structure and function. *Nature Reviews Neuroscience, 10*(6), 410–422. https://doi.org/10.1038/nrn2648

Banotes. (2025, May 15). Bounded rationality and satisficing: A new paradigm in decision. https://banotes.org/administrative-thinkers/bounded-rationality-satisficing-decision-making-simon/

Drury, J. (2018). The role of social identity processes in mass emergency behaviour. *European Review of Social Psychology, 29*(1), 1–47. https://doi.org/10.1080/10463283.2018.1471948

Fiveable. (2024, Aug 16). Bounded rationality and satisficing behavior. https://fiveable.me/intermediate-microeconomic-theory/unit-10/bounded-rationality-satisficing-behavior/study-guide/P3p7Ono0BNkmkCFj

Grupe, D. W., & Nitschke, J. B. (2013). Uncertainty and anticipation in anxiety: An integrated neurobiological and psychological perspective. *Nature Reviews Neuroscience, 14*(7), 488–501. https://doi.org/10.1038/nrn3524

Houston, J. B., Pfefferbaum, B., & Rosenholtz, C. E. (2015). The use of social media during disasters: What can we learn from Hurricane Harvey? *Journal of Emergency Management, 13*(2), 251–260. https://doi.org/10.5055/jem.2015.0236

NTSB. (2010). Loss of thrust in both engines after encountering a flock of birds and subsequent ditching on the Hudson River, US Airways Flight 1549. *Accident Report NTSB/AAR-10/03.* https://www.ntsb.gov/investigations/AccidentReports/Reports/AAR1003.pdf

Roberts, N. P., Kitchiner, N. J., Kenardy, J., & Bisson, J. I. (2014). Systematic review and meta-analysis of multiple-session early interventions following traumatic events. *American Journal of Psychiatry, 166*(3), 293–301. https://doi.org/10.1176/appi.ajp.2008.07081341

Sime, J. D. (2001). Crowd psychology and engineering. *Safety Science, 39*(1), 1–14. https://doi.org/10.1016/S0925-7535(01)00005-4

The Decision Lab. (2021, Oct 11). Bounded rationality. https://thedecisionlab.com/biases/bounded-rationality

Van Bavel, J. J., Baicker, K., Boggio, P. S., et al. (2020). Using social and behavioral science to support COVID-19 pandemic response. *Nature Human Behaviour, 4*, 460–471. https://doi.org/10.1038/s41562-020-0884-z

Weick, K. E., & Sutcliffe, K. M. (2015). Managing the unexpected: Resilient performance in an age of uncertainty. Wiley.

CHAPTER 5

Brandfolder. (2023, April 27). Crisis management examples: Learn from these 7 brands. https://brandfolder.com/resources/crisis-management/

Doodle. (2025, March 23). Crisis leadership and 6 effective examples. https://doodle.com/en/resources/blog/6-examples-of-effective-crisis-leadership/

Drury, J. (2018). The role of social identity processes in mass emergency behaviour. *European Review of Social Psychology, 29*(1), 1–47. https://doi.org/10.1080/10463283.2018.1471948

Dweck, C. S. (2017). Mindset: Changing the way you think to fulfil your potential. Robinson.

Edmondson, A. (2019). The fearless organization: Creating psychological safety in the workplace for learning, innovation, and growth. Wiley.

Edmondson, A. C., & Lei, Z. (2014). Psychological safety: The history, renaissance, and future of an interpersonal construct. *Annual Review of Organizational Psychology and Organizational Behavior, 1*(1), 23–43. https://doi.org/10.1146/annurev-orgpsych-031413-091305

Goleman, D. (1995). Emotional intelligence. Bantam Books.

Highrise. (2023, February 23). Steering the storm: Effective crisis leadership strategies. https://www.tryhighrise.com/blog-posts/crisis-leadership

Houston, J. B., Pfefferbaum, B., & Rosenholtz, C. E. (2015). The use of social media during disasters: What can we learn from Hurricane Harvey? *Journal of Emergency Management, 13*(2), 251–260. https://doi.org/10.5055/jem.2015.0236

Maslow, A. H. (1943). A theory of human motivation. *Psychological Review, 50*(4), 370–396.

NPR. (2012, November 15). Obama visits storm-ravaged New York. https://www.npr.org/sections/thetwo-way/2012/11/15/165197665/obama-visits-storm-ravaged-new-york

Phillips Kaiser. (2024, May 23). The crucial role of empathy in crisis management. https://phillipskaiser.com/crucial-role-of-empathy-in-crisis-management/

Strategy+Business. (2019, October 1). How leaders can bridge the empathy gap in a crisis. https://www.strategy-business.com/blog/How-leaders-can-bridge-the-empathy-gap-in-a-crisis

CHAPTER 6

Abramson, D. M., Grattan, L. M., Mayer, B., Colten, C. E., Arosemena, F. A., Bedimo-Rung, A., & Lichtveld, M. (2015). The resilience activation framework: A conceptual model of how access to social resources promotes adaptation and rapid recovery in post-disaster settings. *The Journal of Behavioral Health Services & Research, 42*(1), 42–57. https://doi.org/10.1007/s11414-014-9410-2

APA. (2020, June 30). Leadership in times of crisis. https://www.apa.org/monitor/2020/07/leadership-crisis

CCL (Center for Creative Leadership). (2025, May 7). Why leadership trust is critical, especially in times of change. https://www.ccl.org/articles/leading-effectively-articles/why-leadership-trust-is-critical-in-times-of-change-and-disruption/

Cialdini, R. B. (2009). Influence: Science and practice (5th ed.). Pearson.

Cocking, C., & Drury, J. (2005). The mass psychology of disasters and emergency evacuations: A research report and implications for planning. University of Sussex.

Drury, J. (2018). The role of social identity processes in mass emergency behaviour. *European Review of Social Psychology, 29*(1), 1–47. https://doi.org/10.1080/10463283.2018.1471948

Edmondson, A. (2019). The fearless organization: Creating psychological safety in the workplace for learning, innovation, and growth. Wiley.

Edmondson, A. C., & Lei, Z. (2014). Psychological safety: The history, renaissance, and future of an interpersonal construct. *Annual Review of Organizational Psychology and Organizational Behavior, 1*(1), 23–43. https://doi.org/10.1146/annurev-orgpsych-031413-091305

Elliott, J. R., & Pais, J. (2006). Race, class, and Hurricane Katrina: Social differences in human responses to disaster. *Social Science Research, 35*(2), 295–321. https://doi.org/10.1016/j.ssresearch.2006.02.003

Goleman, D. (1995). Emotional intelligence. Bantam Books.

PBS. (2016, February 16). Angela Merkel's moral call. https://www.pbs.org/newshour/show/angela-merkels-moral-call

Pennebaker, J. W., & Harber, K. D. (1993). A social stage model of collective coping: The Loma Prieta earthquake and the Persian Gulf War. *Journal of Social Issues, 49*(4), 125–145. https://doi.org/10.1111/j.1540-4560.1993.tb01184.x

Phillips Kaiser. (2024, May 23). The crucial role of empathy in crisis management. https://phillipskaiser.com/crucial-role-of-empathy-in-crisis-management/

Rosenzweig, C., & Solecki, W. (2014). *Hurricane Sandy and adaptation pathways in New York: Lessons from a first-responder city. Global Environmental Change, 28,* 395–408. https://doi.org/10.1016/j.gloenvcha.2014.05.003

Sime, J. D. (2001). Crowd psychology and engineering. *Safety Science, 39*(1), 1–14. https://doi.org/10.1016/S0925-7535(01)00005-4

The Guardian. (2015, October 3). Angela Merkel's bold gamble. https://www.theguardian.com/world/2015/oct/03/angela-merkel-germany-policy-refugees

Van Bavel, J. J., Baicker, K., Boggio, P. S., et al. (2020). Using social and behavioral science to support COVID-19 pandemic response. *Nature Human Behaviour, 4*, 460–471. https://doi.org/10.1038/s41562-020-0884-z

CHAPTER 7

Ambrose, S. E. (1994). *D-Day, June 6, 1944: The climactic battle of World War II.* Simon & Schuster.

Brandfolder. (2023, April 27). Crisis management examples: Learn from these 7 brands. https://brandfolder.com/resources/crisis-management/

Doodle. (2025, March 23). Crisis leadership and 6 effective examples. https://doodle.com/en/resources/blog/6-examples-of-effective-crisis-leadership/

Drury, J. (2018). The role of social identity processes in mass emergency behaviour. *European Review of Social Psychology, 29*(1), 1–47. https://doi.org/10.1080/10463283.2018.1471948

Edmondson, A. (2019). The fearless organization: Creating psychological safety in the workplace for learning, innovation, and growth. Wiley.

Fiveable. (2024, July 24). Adaptive leadership during crises. https://fiveable.me/crisis-management-and-communication/unit-6/adaptive-leadership-crises/study-guide/lsy81O0DIWc4o8ZK

Grupe, D. W., & Nitschke, J. B. (2013). Uncertainty and anticipation in anxiety: An integrated neurobiological and psychological perspective. *Nature Reviews Neuroscience, 14*(7), 488–501. https://doi.org/10.1038/nrn3524

Highrise. (2023, February 23). Steering the storm: Effective crisis leadership strategies. https://www.tryhighrise.com/blog-posts/crisis-leadership

LeadingSapiens. (2025, September 9). Cognitive flexibility: Rewiring how leaders respond. https://www.leadingsapiens.com/cognitive-flexibility/

Risk & Resilience Hub. (2025, September 26). Crisis stress #3: Impact of psychological and cognitive effects. https://riskandresiliencehub.com/crisis-stress-psychological-and-cognitive-effects-impact-decision-making/

SHRM. (2025, January 5). Cognitive flexibility: The science of how to be successful. https://www.shrm.org/executive-network/insights/cognitive-flexibility-science-how-to-successful-business-work

CHAPTER 8

Agile Group. (2025, June 3). Social learning theory and why it matters more than ever. https://agilegroup.co.uk/social-learning-theory-and-why-it-matters-more-than-ever

Bandura, A. (1977). Social learning theory. Prentice Hall.

Bandura, A. (1995). Exercise of personal and collective efficacy in changing societies. In A. Bandura (Ed.), Self-efficacy in changing societies (pp. 1-45). Cambridge University Press.

BBC. (2022, March 7). Ukraine war: President Zelensky defiant in Kyiv as Russian forces close in. https://www.bbc.com/news/world-europe-60618153

Drury, J. (2018). The role of social identity processes in mass emergency behaviour. *European Review of Social Psychology, 29*(1), 1–47. https://doi.org/10.1080/10463283.2018.1471948

DTIC (Defense Technical Information Center). (2023, October). Role modeling resilience via belonging. https://apps.dtic.mil/sti/trecms/pdf/AD1212255.pdf

Edmondson, A. (2019). The fearless organization: Creating psychological safety in the workplace for learning, innovation, and growth. Wiley.

Emerald. (2024, March 18). How leaders' resilient behaviour promotes followers' resilient behaviour. https://www.emerald.com/lodj/article/45/5/754/1218110/Contagious-resilience-how-leaders-resilient

Goleman, D. (1995). Emotional intelligence. Bantam Books.

Gu, Q., & Day, C. (2007). Teachers' resilience: A necessary condition for effectiveness. *Teaching and Teacher Education, 23*(8), 1302–1316. https://doi.org/10.1016/j.tate.2006.06.006

Highrise. (2023, February 23). Steering the storm: Effective crisis leadership strategies. https://www.tryhighrise.com/blog-posts/crisis-leadership

Manz, C. C., & Neck, C. P. (2004). Mastering self-leadership: Empowering yourself for personal excellence (3rd ed.). Pearson.

NYT (New York Times). (2022, March 10). How Zelensky galvanized Ukraine and the world. https://www.nytimes.com/2022/03/10/world/europe/zelensky-ukraine-leadership.html

PositivePsychology. (2025, August 27). Resilience theory: Core concepts & research insights. https://positivepsychology.com/resilience-theory/

Robertson, H. D., Elliott, A. M., Burton, C., Iversen, L., Murchie, P., Porteous, T., & Matheson, C. (2016). Resilience of primary healthcare professionals: A systematic review. *British Journal of General Practice, 66*(647), e423–e433. https://doi.org/10.3399/bjgp16X685261

Snyder, C. R. (1991). In the face of adversity: The power of hope. In C. R. Snyder & D. R. Forsyth (Eds.), *Handbook of social and clinical psychology: The health perspective* (pp. 285–305). Pergamon Press.

Southwick, S. M., Bonanno, G. A., Masten, A. S., Panter-Brick, C., & Yehuda, R. (2014). Resilience definitions, theory, and challenges: Interdisciplinary perspectives. *European Journal of Psychotraumatology, 5*(1), 25338. https://doi.org/10.3402/ejpt.v5.25338

SimplyPsychology. (2025, March 17). Albert Bandura's social learning theory. https://www.simplypsychology.org/bandura.html

CHAPTER 9

Cato Institute. (2025, June 29). Hurricane Katrina: Remembering the federal failures. https://www.cato.org/blog/hurricane-katrina-remembering-federal-failures

Drury, J. (2018). The role of social identity processes in mass emergency behaviour. European Review of Social Psychology, 29(1), 1–47. https://doi.org/10.1080/10463283.2018.1471948

Edmondson, A. (2019). The fearless organization: Creating psychological safety in the workplace for learning, innovation, and growth. Wiley.

Fukushima Investigation Committee. (2012, July 23). Investigation report on the Fukushima nuclear accident.

IAEA. (2015). The Fukushima Daiichi accident: Report by the Director General. https://www-pub.iaea.org/mtcd/publications/pdf/pub1710-reportbythedg-web.pdf

Martinko, M. J., Gundlach, M. J., & Douglas, S. C. (2009). Hurricane Katrina: Lessons in organizational leadership and decision-making. International Journal of Organizational Analysis, 17(1), 80–96. https://doi.org/10.1108/19348830910948921

Sasakawa Peace Foundation. (2024). The Fukushima nuclear accident and crisis management. https://spfusa.org/publications/the-fukushima-nuclear-accident-and-crisis-management/

ShareOK. (2024). The Big Uneasy: Leadership failures in New Orleans in the wake of Hurricane Katrina. https://shareok.org/bitstreams/9d992521-7876-40f0-930a-2af9722b247b/download

Wikipedia. (2005, September 1). Criticism of the government response to Hurricane Katrina. https://en.wikipedia.org/wiki/Criticism_of_the_government_response_to_Hurricane_Katrina

Wikipedia. (2011, March 11). Fukushima nuclear accident. https://en.wikipedia.org/wiki/Fukushima_nuclear_accident

World Nuclear Association. (2024, April 28). Fukushima Daiichi accident. https://world-nuclear.org/information-library/safety-and-security/safety-of-plants/fukushima-daiichi-accident

CHAPTER 10

Bandura, A. (1977). Social learning theory. Prentice Hall.

CompCoRe. (2021). Comparative COVID response. https://compcore.cornell.edu

Doodle. (2025, March 23). Crisis leadership and 6 effective examples. https://doodle.com/en/resources/blog/6-examples-of-effective-crisis-leadership/

Drury, J. (2018). The role of social identity processes in mass emergency behaviour. European Review of Social Psychology, 29(1), 1–47. https://doi.org/10.1080/10463283.2018.1471948

Edmondson, A. (2019). The fearless organization: Creating psychological safety in the workplace for learning, innovation, and growth. Wiley.

Frontiers in Public Health. (2024, January 14). Why do democracies respond differently to COVID-19? https://www.frontiersin.org/articles/10.3389/fpubh.2023.1285552/full

Harvard Kennedy School. (2022, May 15). A comparative perspective on policy responses to COVID-19. https://www.hks.harvard.edu/publications/stress-test-politics-comparative-perspective-policy-responses-covid-19

PMC. (2023, April 21). Pandemic leadership: Is it just a matter of good and bad? https://pmc.ncbi.nlm.nih.gov/articles/PMC10121419/

The Forge. (2025, July 22). Effective leadership in a pandemic: What we learned from COVID-19. https://theforge.defence.gov.au/article/effective-leadership-pandemic-what-we-learned-covid-19-part-2

Van Bavel, J. J., Baicker, K., Boggio, P. S., et al. (2020). Using social and behavioral science to support COVID-19 pandemic response. Nature Human Behaviour, 4, 460–471. https://doi.org/10.1038/s41562-020-0884-z

Wikipedia. (2021, March 11). COVID-19 pandemic by country and territory. https://en.wikipedia.org/wiki/COVID-19_pandemic_by_country_and_territory

CHAPTER 11

Army.mil. (2012, August 19). Public affairs missions is untold 9-11 story. https://www.army.mil/article/65488/public_affairs_missions_is_untold_9_11_story

Bandura, A. (1977). Social learning theory. Prentice Hall.

BBC. (2011, July 25). Norway attacks: PM Jens Stoltenberg urges more democracy. https://www.bbc.com/news/world-europe-14278127

Drury, J. (2018). The role of social identity processes in mass emergency behaviour. *European Review of Social Psychology, 29(1), 1–47.* https://doi.org/10.1080/10463283.2018.1471948

JBA. (2009, September 10). Mayor shows exemplary leadership during 9/11. https://www.jba.af.mil/News/Commentaries/Display/Article/338041/mayor-shows-exemplary-leadership-during-911/

NYT. (2007, September 20). In 9/11 chaos, Giuliani forged a lasting image. https://www.nytimes.com/2007/09/21/us/politics/21giuliani.html

CHAPTER 12

Bandura, A. (1977). Social learning theory. Prentice Hall.

Ben Bernanke. (2015). The courage to act: A memoir of a crisis and its aftermath. W. W. Norton & Company.

Drury, J. (2018). The role of social identity processes in mass emergency behaviour. *European Review of Social Psychology, 29*(1), 1–47. https://doi.org/10.1080/10463283.2018.1471948

Edmondson, A. (2019). The fearless organization: Creating psychological safety in the workplace for learning, innovation, and growth. Wiley.

Greyser, S. A. (1982). Johnson & Johnson: The Tylenol tragedy. Harvard Business School Case 583-043, October 1982.

HBS (Harvard Business School). (2023). The financial crisis of 2008. https://www.hbs.edu/faculty/Pages/item.aspx?num=37144

Harvard Kennedy School. (2022, May 15). A comparative perspective on policy responses to COVID-19. https://www.hks.harvard.edu/publications/stress-test-politics-comparative-perspective-policy-responses-covid-19

Johnson & Johnson. (2015, October 15). Corporate strategy in crisis management: Johnson & Johnson and the Tylenol crisis. https://commons.erau.edu/publication/58/

OU (University of Oklahoma). (1997, December 31). Case study: The Johnson & Johnson Tylenol crisis. https://www.ou.edu/deptcomm/dodjcc/groups/02C2/Johnson%20&%20Johnson.htm

PBS. (2014, September 28). How the Tylenol murders of 1982 changed the way we consume medication. https://www.pbs.org/newshour/health/tylenol-murders-1982

Sciencedirect. (2023). Chicago Tylenol murders: Information and mindfulness. https://www.sciencedirect.com/science/article/abs/pii/S0925753523001327

Wikipedia. (2003, September 28). Chicago Tylenol murders. https://en.wikipedia.org/wiki/Chicago_Tylenol_murders

Wikipedia. (2023). Financial crisis of 2007–2008. https://en.wikipedia.org/wiki/Financial_crisis_of_

CHAPTER 13

AQR International. (2024, May 2). Sir Ernest Shackleton – A 20th Century icon. https://aqrinternational.co.uk/ernest-shackleton-a-model-of-mental-toughness

Bandura, A. (1977). Social learning theory. Prentice Hall.

Climer Consulting. (2023, October 15). Five elements of Shackleton's leadership. https://climerconsulting.com/five-elements-shackletons-leadership/

Drury, J. (2018). The role of social identity processes in mass emergency behaviour. *European Review of Social Psychology, 29*(1), 1–47. https://doi.org/10.1080/10463283.2018.1471948

Edmondson, A. (2019). The fearless organization: Creating psychological safety in the workplace for learning, innovation, and growth. Wiley.

Health Launchpad. (2025, January 26). Leadership lessons from Ernest Shackleton. https://healthlaunchpad.com/leadership-lessons-from-ernest-shackleton/

Shackleton.com. (2021, August 9). Why Ernest Shackleton is still relevant today. https://shackleton.com/blogs/articles/why-ernest-shackleton-is-still-relevant-today

Turvey, J. (2012). Navy SEAL training: Developing resilience and mental toughness. U.S. Naval Institute.

CHAPTER 14

Bavik, Y. L., Tang, P. M., Shao, R., & Lam, L. W. (2021). Team emotional intelligence: Emotional processes as a link between managers and workers. *Journal of Management, 47*(2), 321–347. https://doi.org/10.1177/0149206320921239

Berg, B. L., & Robb, M. (1992). Sympathy strategy: A case study of Johnson & Johnson's Tylenol crisis. *Journal of Public Relations Research, 4*(3), 195–211. https://doi.org/10.1207/s1532754xjprr0403_2

Brandfolder. (2023, April 27). Crisis management examples: Learn from these 7 brands. https://brandfolder.com/resources/crisis-management/

Canterbury District Health Board. (2012). *The initial health-system response to the earthquake in Christchurch, New Zealand, in February 2011.* The Lancet, 379(9818), 2109–2115. https://doi.org/10.1016/S0140-6736(12)60313-4

Center for Creative Leadership. (2025, May 7). How to lead through a crisis. https://www.ccl.org/articles/leading-effectively-articles/how-to-lead-through-a-crisis/

Doodle. (2025, March 23). Crisis leadership and 6 effective examples. https://doodle.com/en/resources/blog/6-examples-of-effective-crisis-leadership/

Drury, J. (2018). The role of social identity processes in mass emergency behavior. *European Review of Social Psychology, 29*(1), 1–47. https://doi.org/10.1080/10463283.2018.1471948

Edmondson, A. (2019). The fearless organization: Creating psychological safety in the workplace for learning, innovation, and growth. Wiley.

Faraj, S., & Xiao, Y. (2006). Coordination in fast response organizations. *Management Science, 52*(8), 1155–1169.

Fink, S. (1983). *Crisis management: Planning for the inevitable.* Harvard Business Review, 61(6), 85–92.

Forbes. (2020, June 30). 4 ways leaders can regulate their emotions at work. https://www.forbes.com/sites/jeremypollack/2020/06/30/4-ways-leaders-can-regulate-their-emotions-at-work/

Goleman, D. (1995). Emotional intelligence. Bantam Books.

Greyser, S. A. (1982). The Tylenol tragedy. *Harvard Business School Case.* https://www.hbs.edu/faculty/Pages/item.aspx?num=17858

Kranz, G. (1999). Eugene F. Kranz oral history. *NASA History Office.* https://historycollection.jsc.nasa.gov/JSCHistoryPortal/history/oral_histories/Kranz EF/KranzEF_4-28-99.htm

Lacerenza, C. N., Marlow, S. L., Tannenbaum, S. I., & Salas, E. (2018). Team development interventions: Evidence-based approaches for improving team

effectiveness. *American Psychologist, 73*(4), 517–531.
https://doi.org/10.1037/amp0000295

Laurillard, D. (2008). Technology enhanced learning as a process of conceptual change. *Journal of Computer Assisted Learning, 24*(5), 370–382.

O'Toole, V. M. (2017). Teachers' reflections and cognitive appraisals in response to the February 2011 Christchurch earthquake. *New Zealand Journal of Psychology, 46*(2), 71–79. https://www.psychology.org.nz/journal-archive/Teachers-reflection-earthquake.pdf

Protecht Group. (2025, April 29). Comprehensive guide to crisis management: Strategies for success. https://www.protechtgroup.com/en-us/blog/comprehensive-crisis-management-guide

Roberts, N. P., Kitchiner, N. J., Kenardy, J., & Bisson, J. I. (2021). Simulation-based training for crisis leadership: Empirical advances and directions. *American Journal of Psychiatry, 178*(3), 214–223.

Tiwari, H. (2015, February 6). Crisis management: Lessons in leadership from Gene Kranz. *LinkedIn.* https://www.linkedin.com/pulse/crisis-management-lessons-leadership-from-gene-kranz-hemlata-tiwari-n4z6c

Tulane School of Social Work. (2024, October 29). Crisis leadership: Skills and strategies. https://socialwork.tulane.edu/blog/crisis-leadership-skills-strategies/

Turvey, J. (2012). Navy SEAL training: Developing resilience and mental toughness. U.S. Naval Institute.

Weaver, S. J., Dy, S. M., & Rosen, M. A. (2010). Team-training in healthcare: A narrative synthesis of the literature. *BMJ Quality & Safety, 19*(6), e49.

CHAPTER 15

Bavik, Y. L., Tang, P. M., Shao, R., & Lam, L. W. (2021). Team emotional intelligence: Emotional processes as a link between managers and workers. *Journal of Management, 47*(2), 321–347. https://doi.org/10.1177/0149206320921239

Center for Creative Leadership. (2025, May 7). How to lead through a crisis. https://www.ccl.org/articles/leading-effectively-articles/how-to-lead-through-a-crisis/

Drury, J. (2018). The role of social identity processes in mass emergency behaviour. *European Review of Social Psychology, 29*(1), 1–47. https://doi.org/10.1080/10463283.2018.1471948

Doodle. (2025, March 23). Crisis leadership and 6 effective examples. https://doodle.com/en/resources/blog/6-examples-of-effective-crisis-leadership/

Edmondson, A. (2019). The fearless organization: Creating psychological safety in the workplace for learning, innovation, and growth. Wiley.

Flin, R. (1996). Sitting in the hot seat: Leaders and teams for critical incident management. Wiley.

Forbes. (2020, June 30). 4 ways leaders can regulate their emotions at work. https://www.forbes.com/sites/jeremypollack/2020/06/30/4-ways-leaders-can-regulate-their-emotions-at-work/

Goleman, D. (1995). Emotional intelligence. Bantam Books.

NYT. (2007, September 20). In 9/11 chaos, Giuliani forged a lasting image. https://www.nytimes.com/2007/09/21/us/politics/21giuliani.html

Protecht Group. (2025, April 29). Comprehensive guide to crisis management: Strategies for success. https://www.protechtgroup.com/en-us/blog/comprehensive-crisis-management-guide

Roberts, N. P., Kitchiner, N. J., Kenardy, J., & Bisson, J. I. (2021). Simulation-based training for crisis leadership: Empirical advances and directions. *American Journal of Psychiatry, 178*(3), 214–223.

Tulane School of Social Work. (2024, October 29). Crisis leadership: Skills and strategies. https://socialwork.tulane.edu/blog/crisis-leadership-skills-strategies/

Weaver, S. J., Dy, S. M., & Rosen, M. A. (2010). Team-training in healthcare: A narrative synthesis of the literature. *BMJ Quality & Safety, 19*(6), e49.

Weick, K. E., & Sutcliffe, K. M. (2015). Managing the unexpected: Resilient performance in an age of uncertainty. Wiley.

CHAPTER 16

Bavik, Y. L., Tang, P. M., Shao, R., & Lam, L. W. (2021). Team emotional intelligence: Emotional processes as a link between managers and workers. *Journal of Management, 47*(2), 321–347. https://doi.org/10.1177/0149206320921239

Center for Creative Leadership (CCL). (2025, May 7). How to lead through a crisis. https://www.ccl.org/articles/leading-effectively-articles/how-to-lead-through-a-crisis/

Drury, J. (2018). The role of social identity processes in mass emergency behaviour. *European Review of Social Psychology, 29*(1), 1–47. https://doi.org/10.1080/10463283.2018.1471948

Doodle. (2025, March 23). Crisis leadership and 6 effective examples. https://doodle.com/en/resources/blog/6-examples-of-effective-crisis-leadership/

Edmondson, A. (2019). The fearless organization: Creating psychological safety in the workplace for learning, innovation, and growth. Wiley.

Goleman, D. (1995). Emotional intelligence. Bantam Books.

Roberts, N. P., Kitchiner, N. J., Kenardy, J., & Bisson, J. I. (2021). Simulation-based training for crisis leadership: Empirical advances and directions. *American Journal of Psychiatry, 178*(3), 214–223.

Weaver, S. J., Dy, S. M., & Rosen, M. A. (2010). Team-training in healthcare: A narrative synthesis of the literature. *BMJ Quality & Safety, 19*(6), e49.

CHAPTER 17

Bavik, Y. L., Tang, P. M., Shao, R., & Lam, L. W. (2021). Team emotional intelligence: Emotional processes as a link between managers and workers. *Journal of Management, 47*(2), 321–347. https://doi.org/10.1177/0149206320921239

Center for Creative Leadership. (2025, May 7). How to lead through a crisis. https://www.ccl.org/articles/leading-effectively-articles/how-to-lead-through-a-crisis/

Drury, J. (2018). The role of social identity processes in mass emergency behaviour. *European Review of Social Psychology, 29*(1), 1–47. https://doi.org/10.1080/10463283.2018.1471948

Edmondson, A. (2019). The fearless organization: Creating psychological safety in the workplace for learning, innovation, and growth. Wiley.

Forbes. (2020, June 30). 4 ways leaders can regulate their emotions at work. https://www.forbes.com/sites/jeremypollack/2020/06/30/4-ways-leaders-can-regulate-their-emotions-at-work/

Goleman, D. (1995). Emotional intelligence. Bantam Books.

Lacerenza, C. N., Marlow, S. L., Tannenbaum, S. I., & Salas, E. (2018). Team development interventions: Evidence-based approaches for improving team effectiveness. *American Psychologist, 73*(4), 517–531. https://doi.org/10.1037/amp0000295

Protecht Group. (2025, April 29). Comprehensive guide to crisis management: Strategies for success. https://www.protechtgroup.com/en-us/blog/comprehensive-crisis-management-guide

Roberts, N. P., Kitchiner, N. J., Kenardy, J., & Bisson, J. I. (2021). Simulation-based training for crisis leadership: Empirical advances and directions. *American Journal of Psychiatry, 178*(3), 214–223.

Weaver, S. J., Dy, S. M., & Rosen, M. A. (2010). Team-training in healthcare: A narrative synthesis of the literature. *BMJ Quality & Safety, 19*(6), e49.

Weick, K. E., & Sutcliffe, K. M. (2015). Managing the unexpected: Resilient performance in an age of uncertainty. Wiley.

CHAPTER 18

Bavik, Y. L., Tang, P. M., Shao, R., & Lam, L. W. (2021). Team emotional intelligence: Emotional processes as a link between managers and workers. *Journal of Management, 47*(2), 321–347. https://doi.org/10.1177/0149206320921239

Center for Creative Leadership (CCL). (2025, May 7). How to lead through a crisis. https://www.ccl.org/articles/leading-effectively-articles/how-to-lead-through-a-crisis/

Drury, J. (2018). The role of social identity processes in mass emergency behaviour. *European Review of Social Psychology, 29*(1), 1–47. https://doi.org/10.1080/10463283.2018.1471948

Doodle. (2025, March 23). Crisis leadership and 6 effective examples. https://doodle.com/en/resources/blog/6-examples-of-effective-crisis-leadership/

Edmondson, A. (2019). The fearless organization: Creating psychological safety in the workplace for learning, innovation, and growth. Wiley.

Goleman, D. (1995). Emotional intelligence. Bantam Books.

Lacerenza, C. N., Marlow, S. L., Tannenbaum, S. I., & Salas, E. (2018). Team development interventions: Evidence-based approaches for improving team effectiveness. *American Psychologist, 73*(4), 517–531. https://doi.org/10.1037/amp0000295

Protecht Group. (2025, April 29). Comprehensive guide to crisis management: Strategies for success. https://www.protechtgroup.com/en-us/blog/comprehensive-crisis-management-guide

Roberts, N. P., Kitchiner, N. J., Kenardy, J., & Bisson, J. I. (2021). Simulation-based training for crisis leadership: Empirical advances and directions. *American Journal of Psychiatry, 178*(3), 214–223.

Weick, K. E., & Sutcliffe, K. M. (2015). Managing the unexpected: Resilient performance in an age of uncertainty. Wiley.

APPENDIX E

Ambrose, S. E. (1994). *D-Day, June 6, 1944: The climactic battle of World War II.* Simon & Schuster.

BBC. (2011, July 25). *Norway attacks: PM Jens Stoltenberg urges 'more democracy'.* BBC News. https://www.bbc.com/news/world-europe-14273011

BBC. (2020, May 8). *Winston Churchill's speeches that inspired Britain.* BBC News. https://www.bbc.com/news/uk-52588297

BBC. (2022, March 4). *Zelensky: Ukraine's wartime president and communicator-in-chief.* BBC News. https://www.bbc.com/news/world-europe-60575927

Bernanke, B. S. (2015). *The courage to act: A memoir of a crisis and its aftermath.* W. W. Norton & Company.

Drury, A. (2018, September 11). *Rudy Giuliani and the legacy of 9/11 leadership. Time Magazine.* https://time.com/longform/rudy-giuliani-9-11-legacy

Doodle. (2025). *Leadership under fire: Profiles in calm command.* Doodle Leadership Institute. https://www.doodleleadership.org

Harvard Business School (HBS). (2023). *Leadership in crisis: The 2008 financial meltdown.* Harvard Business School Publishing. https://hbr.org

New York Times (NYT). (2007, September 9). *Rudy Giuliani's leadership after 9/11. The New York Times.* https://www.nytimes.com

New York Times (NYT). (2022, March 1). *Zelensky's wartime messages unite Ukraine and the world. The New York Times.* https://www.nytimes.com

NPR. (2012, December 16). *Obama's remarks at Sandy Hook interfaith vigil. NPR.* https://www.npr.org

OU. (1997). *The Tylenol crisis, 1982: Johnson & Johnson's response.* Oklahoma University Center for Business Ethics.

PBS. (2014, October 5). *Tylenol murders: The crisis that changed product safety. PBS Frontline.* https://www.pbs.org/wgbh/frontline/article/tylenol-murders

PBS. (2016, September 5). *Angela Merkel: Leadership and the refugee crisis. PBS NewsHour.* https://www.pbs.org/newshour

Shackleton.com. (2021). *Sir Ernest Shackleton: Leadership and endurance.* https://www.shackleton.com

The Guardian. (2015, September 10). *Angela Merkel: 'Wir schaffen das' – the phrase that defined a crisis. The Guardian.* https://www.theguardian.com

Turvey, B. (2012). *The psychology of crisis leadership: Lessons from Navy SEAL training.* Naval Leadership Review. https://www.navyleadershipreview.mil

Reader's Notes

Reader's Notes

Reader's Notes

Reader's Notes

ABOUT THE AUTHOR

Dr. Frazer G. Thompson is a seasoned entertainment executive, crisis responder, and storyteller with almost three decades of experience at the intersection of public safety, themed attractions and human behavior. His leadership roles at major themed entertainment companies have shaped his approach to the guest experience, cross-functional team dynamics, and crisis readiness. Subsequently, Dr. Thompson has spent time in Israel researching human success factors, resilience, and public space design under duress. In his current role, he is responsible for the preparedness, trauma-informed training, and narrative-led approach that prioritizes empathy, clarity, and connection of security with guest and employee safety. He is an addiction specialist and the author and co-author of several works on leadership, memory, and meaning in high-pressure environments. He is also a contributing writer for JCAT First Responders Toolbox publications, in conjunction with the NCTC, DHS, and FBI.

www.ingramcontent.com/pod-product-compliance
Lightning Source LLC
Chambersburg PA
CBHW062246270326
41931CB00026B/1735